"LIGHTENED WITH HIS GLORY"

"LIGHTENED WITH HIS GLORY"

ROBERT J. WIELAND

CFI Book Division
Gordonsville, Tennessee

3

Unless otherwise noted Bible quotations are from the King James Version, copyright ©1988, B. B. Kirkebride Bible Company, Inc., Indianapolis, Indiana, used by permission.
NEB *The New English Bible* © copyright 1970 by Oxford University Press. Used by permission. All rights reserved.
NIV *The Holy Bible, New International Version* © 1978 by International Bible Society, Zondervan Bible Publishers. Used by permission. All rights reserved.
LB *The Living Bible* paraphrase © 1974 by Tyndale House Publishers, Inc. Used by permission. All rights reserved.

Published by CFI Book Division

P.O. Box 159, Gordonsville, Tennessee 38563

ISBN: 978-1-7344387-0-3

Printed in the United States of America

Typeset in 11.5/13.8 Minion Pro

"And after these things I saw another angel come down from heaven, having great power; and the earth was lightened with his glory. And he cried mightily with a strong voice, saying, 'Babylon the great is fallen, is fallen, and is become the habitation of devils, and the hold of every foul spirit, and a cage of every unclean and hateful bird. For all nations have drunk of the wine of the wrath of her fornication, and the kings of the earth have committed fornication with her, and the merchants of the earth are waxed rich through the abundance of her delicacies.' And I heard another voice from heaven, saying, 'Come out of her, My people, that ye be not partakers of her sins, and that ye receive not of her plagues.'" Revelation 18:1-4.

CONTENTS

INTRODUCTION
Why Is This Subject Important?

The history and content of the 1888 message are of keen interest to Seventh-day Adventists around the world. Ellen White has said repeatedly that failure to understand and to accept that message has greatly retarded the progress of the church and delayed the triumph of the "everlasting gospel" message.

In our modern day, schisms, apostasies, fanaticisms, conflicting interpretations of the prophecies, and the inroads of the so-called "new theology," have plagued the church. The resultant loss of ministers and members has been heavy. These many problems are related to confusion and misconception of the 1888 history and message.

Those who believe the New Testament recognize that the Jews rejected and crucified their Messiah. If the Jewish nation should wish to get right with God, would it not be a good idea for them to understand that mistake and repent of it?

If we wish to get right with the Lord, would it not be wise for us to understand our history and accept His gift of repentance? "We have nothing to fear for the future, except as we shall forget the way the Lord has led us, and His teaching in our past history" (Ellen G. White, *Life Sketches*, p. 196). It would follow logically that we have everything to fear if we forget our past and disregard "His teaching in our past history."

It is encouraging to remember that Jesus promised that "ye shall know the truth, and the truth shall make you free." As we near the end of time, more and more truth will come to light, for Jesus said, "All power is given to me in heaven and in earth." Every truth-seeker in the world can be comforted by His assurance that if we ask for bread, He will never give us a stone.

Especially in respect of the heartwarming "1888 message," a growing number of scores of thousands of Seventh-day Adventists in many countries are now discovering that it is indeed what Ellen White said it is, "most precious." They love its Good News. It has renewed their confidence in the Lord's leading and in the future triumph of His work. They see the leading of the Lord in the history of this church, and are encouraged to believe that He will bring the good ship that bears the people of God safely into port. Many testify that this message has saved them from leaving the church in discouragement.

Best of all, the "1888 message" is glorious good news of salvation through faith alone, a message of deliverance from the controlling power of sin, a message of spiritual hope. It is a clearer understanding of the "everlasting gospel" as it is related to the unique Adventist truth of the cleansing of the sanctuary. It is a truth which has been entrusted to Seventh-day Adventists. "This is the message that God commanded to be given to the world" (*Testimonies to Ministers and Gospel Workers*, page 92).t

Can all the powers of hell prevent this message going to the ends of the earth as the Lord commanded that it should go? The answer is no. Nevertheless, there are questions, perplexities, and objections that sincere people have. These we wish to consider.

QUESTIONS ABOUT THE 1888 MESSAGE

Why is the gospel so important?

A true understanding of the gospel is precisely what this sin-cursed world desperately needs to know. After Christianity has professed to proclaim the gospel for two thousand years, the agony and evil in the world appear to be getting worse. Millions who want to believe in God feel forced to doubt that He exists or that He cares. Could it be that the pure gospel has not yet been proclaimed as it should be?

Surprising as it may be, there is more than one gospel: (1) the pure truth that Paul and the apostles preached which he calls "the grace of Christ," and (2) there is a counterfeit gospel which he says is "another gospel: which is not another," but a perversion of "the gospel of Christ." According to Paul's strong words, "any other gospel" than the true one Christ gave ends up being a "curse" (Galatians 1:6-9).

The reason why the enemy of Christ specializes in perverting the gospel is because he knows that the true one is "the power of God unto salvation" (Romans 1:16), just as good food is healthful nourishment to one's body. But a little arsenic mixed in one's diet is lethal. In the final judgment all will see that the world's continual agony has been the direct result of a perversion of the gospel which "Babylon" has foisted on mankind (Revelation 18:24).

Do Seventh-day Adventists have something special to do in recovering that pure gospel?

Many of us have assumed that the popular Evangelical churches proclaim the gospel to the world, and our special task is to proclaim the law. The idea has been that if we add to their "gospel" our unique understanding of the Ten Commandments along with the Sabbath, then we come up with the "third angel's message." In other words,

Seventh-day Adventists are just one church among many with no distinct message other than a special list of things people must learn to do if they wish to be saved.

The truth is that the Lord has given us a special message of Good News people must learn to *believe*. The Lord never called Seventh-day Adventists to preach legalism to the world. Our special commission is to recover and proclaim the precise Good News that is already "the salvation of God" and which prepares a people for the second coming of Christ. In fact, the message of the three angels of Revelation 14:6-12 is in a unique sense "the everlasting gospel" for the last days. It must be the best Good News the world will ever hear.

How does the 1888 message fit in with our special task?

"The Lord in His great mercy sent" it as "the beginning" of the loud cry message of Revelation 18:1-4 (*Testimonies to Ministers and Gospel Workers*, pages 91-93; *Review and Herald*, November 22, 1892). Ellen White often recognized this as its true identity (cf. Letter B2A, 1892; MS 15, 1888, etc). Never did she say that it was a mere re-emphasis of what the pioneers had always believed, or of what the Protestant Evangelical churches teach.

She also identified the 1888 message as "showers of the latter rain from heaven" (*Special Testimonies*, Series A, No. 6, page 19). She had already stated that the latter rain would come either as a preparation for the loud cry or simultaneously with it (*Early Writings*, page 271; MS 15, 1888). Never did she identify any other message at any other time as the latter rain. She could not have said that the loud cry began with the 1888 message of Christ and His righteousness unless the latter rain had come at the same time.

The latter rain and the loud cry are to the church today what the birth of the Messiah in Bethlehem was to the Jews. For many decades we have been praying for the Lord to give us this gift of the latter rain, as the Jews prayed for their Messiah to come. They were to find the fulfillment of their destiny in Him. But they did not receive Him (John 1:11). Likewise this church is to find the fulfillment of its destiny in the latter rain and the loud cry that began more than a century and a quarter ago.

What is meant by "loud cry" and "latter rain"?

The three angels of Revelation 14:6-12 proclaim a worldwide message, but the original Greek gives the picture of their flying "in the midst of heaven" like a helicopter flying over the tree-tops. The past 175 years of history indicate to a candid observer that their message has so far attained only a limited penetration of the world.

But the fourth angel of Revelation 18 comes down "having great power, and the earth [is] lightened with his glory." This angel comes like a great space ship with light that envelopes the whole world. He cries "mightily with a strong voice." Here at last is total, final penetration with the message.

Because God is love and must be fair to everyone, His Good News message must go everywhere before Christ can return. An inspired messenger tells us that the mark of the beast "is to be presented in some shape to every institution and every individual" (*Selected Messages*, book 3, page 396). To be fair, God must see to it that the warning message has equal penetration.

The "latter rain" is the final outpouring of the Holy Spirit. It will empower God's people to be His witnesses in the last conflict of the ages. Although the "former rain" at Pentecost was glorious, we are told that the final outpouring will be far greater in scope.

What is the most important subject of the 1888 message?

It is primarily a "revelation of the righteousness of Christ, the sin-pardoning Redeemer" (*Review and Herald*, November 22, 1892). It proclaims "justification through faith in the Surety, ... the righteousness of Christ" (*Testimonies to Ministers and Gospel Workers*, pages 91, 92). In reading through the hundreds of Ellen White's endorsements of the message from 1888 through 1896 (see Appendix), one is impressed with her overwhelming conviction that it was "the beginning" of a final revelation of the gospel of righteousness by faith. It was to be more clear and powerful than our people (or the world) had heard, at least since the days of Paul.

One statement goes so far as to say that it was the beginning of light not clearly seen since *before* Paul's day, that is, since Pentecost (*Fundamentals of Christian Education*, page 473; cf. *Review and Herald*, June 3, 1890). In other words, even Paul could learn something from "the third angel's message in verity."

There were other ancillary aspects of the message, such as health reform, educational and organizational reform, etc. But what rejoiced Ellen White's heart repeatedly was the much more abounding grace in its righteousness by faith message. It's easy to see that her hundreds of endorsements are overwhelmingly concerned with that aspect of the message.

I have heard it often said that the 1888 message was only "a re-emphasis" of the preaching of Martin Luther, John Calvin, the Wesleys, and the popular evangelists of the 19th century such as Dwight L. Moody and Charles Spurgeon. Is this true?

A study of the actual content of the 1888 message reveals very marked differences with that of the 16th-century Protestant Reformers and the Evangelicals of the 19th-century or even of today.

Ellen White recognized those differences. She said that the 1888 message of righteousness by faith is "the third angel's message in verity" (*Review and Herald*, April 1, 1890). This is a problem to some of our people, for the general idea has been that there is only one kind of righteousness by faith, that which the Evangelicals teach.

But the problem can easily be solved by asking one simple question: did Luther, Calvin, the Wesleys, and the Sunday-keeping Evangelicals of her day proclaim "the third angel's message"?

If the answer is yes, we have no denominational foundation and there is no reason for this church to exist. Logically, the popular "re-emphasis" view says this, and has created the confusion which has caused many pastors and members to leave the church. If the Evangelicals preach the true gospel of righteousness by faith, why not join them?

So far as we know, Ellen White never took her pen to characterize the 1888 message as a "re-emphasis" of the gospel others had taught. In fact, she said it was "the first clear teaching on this subject from any human lips" that she had ever heard proclaimed publicly (MS 5, 1889).

Doubtless there were some minor aspects of the message that others had always proclaimed; but she recognized a new and distinct perspective never before clearly seen. Like a picture more sharply focused, "great truths that [had] lain unheeded and unseen since the day of Pentecost [began] to shine from God's word in their native purity" (*Fundamentals of Christian Education*, page 473). This is why

14

she identified the message as "the beginning" of the latter rain and the loud cry, light which had never before lightened the earth with glory.

If we accept the righteousness-by-faith message of the popular Sunday-keeping churches of today ("Evangelical Christianity") will that not suffice as a substitute for the 1888 message?

If the 1888 message "is the third angel's message in verity," it is obvious that Evangelical concepts cannot substitute for it, because the popular Sunday-keeping churches are not proclaiming the message of the seal of God and the mark of the beast. In fact, the genuine justification by faith message of 1888 "is made manifest in obedience to all the commandments of God" (*Testimonies to Ministers and Gospel Workers*, page 92). That must include observance of the fourth commandment! Yet the Evangelical churches have generally opposed the Sabbath and sanctuary truths for the entire period of Seventh-day Adventist existence. Something somewhere does not add up.

There are fundamental truths of the atonement, the cross, the meaning of genuine love and faith, the motivation to obedience, that are either absent from Evangelical "righteousness by faith" or are seriously distorted there. The very finest Evangelical minds are not wrestling with the real problem of the atonement. Why have 2000 years of history elapsed since the grand event of the cross which they say was the final victory? Other than by Calvinist predeterminism, they are helpless to explain why this long delay continues.

Ancient Israel was constantly tempted and enticed by the counterfeit doctrines of her neighbors. Those pagan ideas were superficially similar. One such was Baal worship. If the Lord has entrusted the third angel's message to Seventh-day Adventists, we must also face in principle the same temptation to be confused by a counterfeit. Somehow a clearer truth of the cross of Christ must emerge than has been presented by the Sunday-keeping churches.

For many decades we have heard righteousness by faith preached in our churches, camp meetings, and workers' meetings. How does the 1888 message differ from what we have already heard all these many years?

There are many fresh, beautiful truths in it that are not usually understood today. For example:

(1) *The revelation of the nearness of the Saviour.* This is what Ellen White termed "the message of Christ's righteousness." Righteousness means something different than "holiness." At His birth, He was "that holy thing" (Luke 1:35). But as He grew to manhood and finally came to His cross, Christ developed a character of "righteousness." Holiness denotes the character of one who in a sinless nature is holy. Thus we read of the "holy angels." Never do we read of "righteous angels."

Righteousness describes the character of one who has taken a *sinful* human nature but has resisted and conquered sin. Thus the phrase "Christ our righteousness" means that Christ "overcame" and "condemned sin" in the same fallen, sinful nature that we have. He came so close to us 2000 years ago and ever since that He has "condemned sin in the flesh" (cf. Revelation 3:21; Romans 8:3). Since the Father and the Son are one and the Father was in Christ during His incarnation experience, the Father is also spoken of as "righteous."

Christ has made sin to become passé. There is no excuse for it any longer. He truly became one of us, 100 percent God, yet also 100 percent human. He "took upon His sinless nature our sinful nature" (*Medical Ministry*, p. 181), so He can save every one of us *from* our sins, not in them. He knows how we are tempted, for He was "in all points tempted like as we are, yet without sin" (Hebrews 4:15).

This Good News grips human hearts. In it lies the truth that explains the reason for the 2000-year delay in the return of Christ that the popular churches do not comprehend.

(2) *Christ's closing sanctuary ministry of the final atonement.* Here is where the nature-of-Christ truth shines brightest and transcends sterile theological argument. The Book of Revelation shows us a people who at last are the "firstfruits" of Christ's sacrifice and who stand before His throne "without fault" (14:5-12). The key to their victory lies in their overcoming *even as He overcame* (3:21).

Here the truth of the nature of Christ comes into its own. The High Priest's ministry in the Most Holy Apartment since 1844 is a grand truth yet to lighten the earth and bring into sharp focus the closing issues of the great controversy (*Evangelism*, pages 221, 222). Our Seventh-day Adventist identity rests on that sanctuary-truth foundation, yet it is common knowledge that it is all but lost in our contemporary preaching. And our Evangelical brethren teach no concept of that Day of Atonement ministry.

(3) *The 1888 message joins justification by faith to that special closing work of atonement.* This is why Ellen White saw it to be distinctly and uniquely "the third angel's message in verity." She rejoiced to recognize the long-awaited connection.

In the early months of 1890 she wrote a series of articles in the *Review* that demonstrated how this message is the essence of the cleansing of the sanctuary truth (January 21 through June 3).

(4) *The message is not a stern "get-ready-or-else" demand, but glorious Good News of how to get ready.* It transforms Adventist imperatives into gospel enablings. It reveals the Saviour as a Divine Physician of souls, a "nigh-at-hand" Healer of every wound that sin has caused in the human psyche. He is the grand, effective Original of every stop-gap, 12-point program devised by experts to meet the desperate need of addicts of every kind from alcoholics to shopaholics. It is also the only hope for saints addicted to worldly lukewarmness.

It was Heaven's intention that addicts of every kind "shall [find] deliverance ... in the remnant" rather than in worldly programs (cf. Joel 2:32). Seventh-day Adventists were called to be "foremost" in uplifting a real Saviour who was tempted in all points like as every addict on earth is tempted, *yet without sin.* Thus He can save to the uttermost.

(5) *Assurance of salvation comes with the 1888 truth of justification by faith.* Calvinism says that Christ died only for the elect. While Arminianism protests that He died for "all men," it also says that He merely made a "provision" whereby it *might be possible* for "all men" to be justified *if* they take the initiative in doing something right first. If the sinner does not take advantage of the "offer," then the death of Christ on the cross has done and will do him no good. This is the general idea our people have had.

The 1888 messengers saw that the cross accomplished far more than making a mere provision which is dependent on the sinner's initiative. Christ has done something for every human being! "All men" owe even *this present life* to the sacrifice of Christ. Human salvation depends on God's initiative, and damnation depends on man's initiative. When the sinner hears the Good News and believes, he responds to God's initiative, and thus he experiences justification by faith.

Here is where the 1888 idea of justification by faith exposes subtle legalism. In pure New Testament justification by faith "boasting ... is excluded" (Romans 3:27), but in the popular view the key factor is the sinner's initiative. He can say, "*I* took advantage of the offer, *I* accepted the provision, *I* made the decision that brings me to heaven. Christ's sacrifice did me no good until *I* did something about it." Thus an egocentric mindset is locked in, and a subliminal legalism remains.

Something is tragically missing in this idea. Bible truth is that Christ actually "tasted" the second death "for every man," and made propitiation for the "sins of the whole world" (Romans 3:24, 25; Hebrews 2:9; 1 John 2:2). The sins of "all men" were legally imputed unto Him as He died so that no one has as yet had to bear the true burden of his guilt (Romans 5:16-18; 2 Corinthians 5:19).

Therefore "all men" live because He died for them, whether or not they believe (vss. 14, 15). Not only at Easter when people eat hot cross buns, but *every loaf of bread is "stamped" with the cross*. This means that both saints and sinners are "daily" equally nourished by the sacrifice of Christ (*The Desire of Ages*, page 660). He has brought life and immortality to light through the gospel (2 Timothy 1:10). For whom has He brought life? For "all men." For whom has He also brought immortality? For those who believe.

Therefore, since "all men" live because their trespasses were imputed unto One who died in their place, it is correct to say that a legal justification has been effected for all men. (Some prefer the term "corporate justification" or "forensic justification." The truth is the same.) As "all men" are under legal "condemnation" "in Adam" by birth, so Christ has become the "last Adam" in whom the entire human race are legally acquitted (1 Corinthians 15:22; Romans 5:16-18, *The New English Bible*). This is the "in Christ" idea of the New Testament.

This *does not* mean that "all men" will be saved against their will. The gift Christ has given "every man" can be despised and refused. He will not force anyone to believe. But the 1888 messengers maintained that *when* the sinner hears and *believes* this Good News, his experience of justification *by faith* forthwith makes him "obedient to all the commandments of God," including the Sabbath commandment. This is the only possible result of a sinner laying hold of Christ's righteousness by an intelligent, informed faith. No wonder Ellen White rejoiced when she first heard the message.

Thus the 1888 message recognizes what truth there is in both Calvinism and Arminianism, but goes far beyond both. As Calvinism rightly discerns, the sinner's salvation is due entirely to God's initiative. As Arminianism rightly discerns, all men have an equal *possibility* of salvation. But as neither discerns, Christ has borne the sins of "all men," and has died the second death for "every man." He has taken the initiative to save "every man." The only reason any sinner can be lost therefore is because he has taken the initiative to *despise and reject* the justification already given him and placed in his hands (see John 3:16-19; 12:48).

Thus the 1888 message sees sin in a far more serious light than most Adventists see it. It is not a passive do-nothingness. Sin is so terrible that it constantly resists and rejects the saving grace of God. The sinner doesn't realize what he is doing, and must be told. Only in this light can repentance be seen and appreciated in its true dimensions.

(6) *The Holy Spirit is far more powerful than we have thought.* When one understands and believes how good the Good News is, then he sees that it is easy to be saved and hard to be lost.

Salvation is not dependent on our seeking and finding God (the root element of every pagan religion in the world), but on our believing that He is seeking and has found us. The Holy Spirit is stronger than the flesh (Galatians 5:16, 17), and grace much more abounds than abounding sin (Romans 5:20).

(7) *In other words, the 1888 message lifts the love of God as Saviour far above the merely provisional category.* The 1888 message does not present Him as casually giving the sinner a take-it-or-leave-it offer, "Too bad for you if you don't take advantage of the bargain." Christ is seen as a Good Shepherd who is actively seeking His lost sheep "until he find it" (Luke 15:4). The sinner must hear the Good News.

God's love is immeasurably clarified by the Biblical concepts in the 1888 message. The only possible result: a replacement of dead works by a heart-felt service of faith, a devotion that knows no limit. Lukewarmness becomes impossible to one who understands and believes that pure gospel.

(8) *The heart-changing power of the two-covenants truth.* This unique 1888 concept is not understood well in the church today, nor in modern Evangelicalism. Ellen White "was shown" that the Lord gave the 1888 messengers the correct view (Letters 30, 59, 1890).

This again is not a theological puzzle. It is practical godliness. Paul says that a wrong idea of the covenants "gendereth to bondage" (Galatians 4:24). Not knowing what we are doing, we have taught children and youth the old covenant ideas for decades. It results in many losing their way spiritually. When the 1888 view of the two covenants is compared with the view generally taught among us today, it is no wonder that a large number of our youth don't understand the gospel, and that we lose so many of them.

Again, like an inadequate view of justification, the non-1888 view opens the door to a self-centered motivation—the essence of legalism. We are not saved by making promises to God, but by believing His promises to us. (A re-discovery of the 1888 idea of the two covenants was the spark that generated the present revival of interest in this message.)

(9) *A correct motivation for serving Christ is another term for the dynamic of genuine justification by faith.* The *legal* justification was achieved at the cross for "all men"; this is *objective*. The *experience* of justification by faith motivates the believer to complete devotion to Christ; this is *subjective*. All self-centered motivation involves legalism. To be "under grace" is to realize the higher motivation imposed by a heart appreciation of the grace of Christ. This delivers from the lesser motivations of fear of hell or hope of reward (cf. Romans 6:14, 15; *The Desire of Ages*, page 480).

While the 1888 message is glorious Good News to those who appreciate the cross of Christ, it opens up the possibility of very Bad News for Adventists who are unconscious of their true spiritual condition. To be "under the law" is the opposite of being "under grace." This is why legalism is the true essence of all motivation imposed by fear of being lost or desire for reward. But there is a remedy. "Perfect love (*agape*) casteth out fear" (1 John 4:18).

Our superficial "assurance-of-salvation" concern appears childish in comparison, but the 1888 concept of grace makes possible a deliverance from this deeper root of selfishness. It enables the believer to share a total closeness with Christ, to be "incorporate" with Him, the *ego* being "crucified with Him." Paul frequently addresses the "believers incorporate in Christ Jesus." He says that "we have become incorporate with Him in a death like His" (Ephesians 1:1; Romans 6:5, *The New English Bible,* etc.).

Anything short of this is an immature "righteousness by faith," suitable only for the flower girl at the wedding. A true bride has a higher concern—the honor and vindication of her Bridegroom, for she has at last become "incorporate" in him.

(10) *Thus the 1888 idea of "perfection" is not a fear-oriented grasping for security, but a Christ-centered concern for Him to receive His reward.* No longer is overcoming degraded to a topic for theological arguments, forcing Ellen White's words into mind-twisting contradictions.

Granted, a true "under grace" motivation is impossible for any sinful human apart from the revelation of Christ's sacrifice. But to "glory in the cross" is an experience that is possible for any sinner who will behold and believe. A people can be prepared for the coming of Christ!

Should we claim "verbal inspiration" for Jones and Waggoner? Or "fixate" on their words?

No, neither can a claim of "verbal inspiration" be made for the actual words of the Bible or of the Spirit of Prophecy writings. The value of a message is the light that is in it, the concepts that illuminate truths of the everlasting gospel that have been so lost sight of. No one claims any more for Jones and Waggoner than Ellen White herself claimed for them. She said that they were "the Lord's delegated messengers" who had "heavenly credentials" (see Appendix).

The message of Jones and Waggoner as found in their available books and articles contains its own credentials. It appeals to people today because its basic concepts are so refreshingly different that they still come as "new light." And they were only "the beginning" of the "loud cry" light that must eventually penetrate everywhere.

Although we need fresh servings of "the bread of life" for today, when Jesus fed the 5000 He told His disciples, "Gather up the fragments that remain, that nothing be lost" (John 6:12). If the Lord "sent" the 1888 message, we must gather up the "fragments" that His providence has left for us. Surely the time has come for God's people around the world to think seriously. Is it not irreverent for us to demand of the Lord more light when we criticize and reject what He has already sent us?

The 1888 message spoke to a different culture than we face today. How can this century-old message help us meet the needs of secular-minded people who no longer believe in God or the Bible?

Modern man has encased himself spiritually in a subterranean bunker with secular walls 12 feet thick. But the Holy Spirit has one cruise missile that can penetrate those walls: the *agape* message of the cross of Christ.

This does not mean that other aspects of the Adventist message are no longer valid. It is still true that health reform is the "right arm of the message," and helps to break down prejudice. Church fellowship helps to meet people's social needs. Church-sponsored education provides (at least to some extent) a refuge for children and youth. Our 28 fundamental beliefs give cohesion to our religious philosophy. *But persuading modern secular man to join our religious club is not lighting the earth with the glory of the gospel.* The same ego-orientation can prevail within our "club" as without.

What is needed is Good News that will lighten a world dark with misapprehension of God, and reconcile alienated secular hearts to Him.

That message is an understanding of the love of God that transcends the concepts of modern Babylon. "The third angel's message in verity" that came to us in 1888 is the "beginning" of that message. In essence it is a revelation of a love beyond usual understanding. Nothing less than the full disclosure of that love in its "breadth, and length, and depth, and height" can suffice. The "loud cry" will not be a terror' inducing appeal to raw fear but a last-days' "revelation of [God's] character of love" (*Christ's Object Lessons*, page 415).

For example, if we make the reality of *agape* clear to an atheistic evolutionist, we can ask him where he thinks such a totally radical idea could have come from. He will have to answer—its only origin is a cross on a lonely hill at a place called Calvary.

"... the unparalleled love of Christ, through the agency of the Holy Spirit, will bring conviction and conversion to the hardened heart" (A. G. Daniells, *Christ Our Righteousness*, page 61). In a previously unknown statement Ellen White adds: "For years I have seen that there is a broken link which has kept us from reaching hearts, this link is supplied by presenting the love and mercy of God" (*Remarks to Presidents*, March 3, 1891; General Conference Archives).

No other people can lift up the cross as can Seventh-day Adventists if we will humble our hearts to receive the light that the Lord sent us. This is because no other people have an understanding both of the nature of man and of the nature of Christ as the Lord has wanted to give that understanding to us.

Secular people living in this last century of the Christian era need the same message that the Lord sent to the pagans during its first century—Christ and Him crucified. The apostles spoke the language of their day; we shall speak the language of our day. But that same proclamation of the cross still challenges the thinking of modern man, and penetrates the defenses in which he has encased his worldly heart.

"Historic Adventism" generates fear of the investigative judgment. Does the 1888 message provide a solution to this problem?

It is true that such fear has shadowed the church for decades. Roger L. Dudley documents among academy youth its recurring idea (*Why Teenagers Reject Religion and What to Do About It*, Review and Herald Publishing Association, pages 9-21, 1978). Marvin Moore in *The Refiner's Fire* (Pacific Press Publishing Association, 2014) recognizes how general is the problem, and sincerely seeks a solution.

The apostle John declares that wherever we find fear, its presence betrays the absence of *agape*, for "perfect love [*agape*] casts out fear" (1 John 4:18). It would be impossible for such fear to grip our youth in the 1990s if we had accepted "the most precious message" in the 1888 era and since. That special love, *agape*, is the basic idea of the message.

The solution to the problem of fear is revealing the true Christ who came in the "likeness of sinful flesh, and for sin, condemned sin in the flesh." The liberating truth is seen thus: "Forasmuch then as the children are partakers of flesh and blood, he also himself likewise took part of the same; that through death he might destroy him that had the power of death, that is, the devil; and deliver them *who through fear of death were all their lifetime subject to bondage*" (Hebrews 2:14, 15).

But how does this message deliver from fear?

All its aspects focused on the reality of what happened on the cross. That "revelation" was like the sun's rays passing through a glass—it ignited fire that burns fear out of human hearts.

A distinct contribution of Adventism to the message of the cross is that Christ died the equivalent of the second death, the death in which He surrendered all hope of resurrection (cf. *The Desire of Ages*, page 753). When fear-filled human hearts see the true Christ in that "revelation" of *agape*, they identify with Him in such a way that self is "crucified with Christ," and the believer becomes "incorporate" in Him, as Paul says. The union is as close as that of a bride with her husband. We "let this mind be in [us] which was also in Christ Jesus" (Philippians 2:5). The believer becomes one with the crucified Lord.

Realizing, seeing, the reality of His descent into hell in order to save our souls, how He faced that utter annihilation of hope, how He chose to go down into eternal darkness, to endure the eternal hiding of His Father's face in order to redeem us—this union with Him stretches our dwarfed human hearts outsize so that we can *begin* to understand the price that it cost Him to save us. We can never duplicate His sacrifice, but we *can appreciate* it. We "survey the wondrous cross, on which the Prince of glory died." This eradicates fear from the heart.

The reason is this: since no fear can be as great as the fear of hell, if that fear is conquered by appreciating His sacrifice through fellowship with Him on His cross, all lesser fears have to be dissipated.

For example, how could the penitent thief on the cross ever again be tormented with fear? For anyone else who has been "crucified with Christ," the same deliverance must take place. There is no fear left in the entire universe that can survive a heart-union with Him in that hour of the cross. But again it must be said that the true dimensions of that sacrifice are comprehended only in the light of "the third angel's message in verity."

This was the impact of the 1888 message. It recovered Paul's grand obsession: "The [*agape*] of Christ constraineth us; because we thus judge, that if one died for all, then were all dead" (2 Corinthians 5:14). How can one who knows he is "dead" ever again be afraid of anything? How can one who has already been to hell (through being crucified with Christ) ever again fear anything less than hell?

But isn't the Adventist fear of the investigative judgment precisely that—the fear of hell?

Yes, without the 1888 idea it is dominated by that fear. For "self" to be crucified with Christ does not mean a human effort to torture ourselves by an agonizing do-it-yourself crucifixion. It is always "with Christ." The message of the cross "constrains ... henceforth" to a life of service to Christ free from fear: "He died for all, that they which live should not henceforth live unto themselves, but unto him which died for them and rose again" (verse 15).

When Paul says "I am crucified with Christ" he is not saying, "See what a strong Christian I am! I am nailing nails through my hands and feet, I am crucifying myself!" Rather he is saying,

When I survey the wondrous cross
On which the Prince of glory died,
My richest gain I count but loss,
And pour contempt on all my pride.
                    —*Isaac Watts*

He is saying, "My proud self is already 'crucified with Him.' Self cannot live and reign any longer because His *agape* has annihilated the love of self. And since self is now crucified with Him, fear is gone because fear always feeds on the love of self."

The 1888 message focused the doctrine of the investigative judgment into its proper perspective, introducing a concern for Christ rather than for our own personal salvation. This is why Ellen White united the 1888 message of justification by faith with the investigative judgment truth in that special series of articles in the *Review and Herald* during the early months of 1890.

But here is an Ellen White quotation that has always worried me—The Great Controversy, page 425. Why did Ellen White say such a fearful thing?

Perhaps you have misunderstood the statement. Let us see what it actually says:

> Says the prophet: "Who may abide the day of His coming? and who shall stand when He appeareth? for He is like a refiner's fire, and like fullers' soap: and He shall sit as a refiner and purifier of silver: and He shall purify the sons of Levi, and purge them as gold and silver, that they may offer unto the Lord an offering in righteousness." Malachi 3:2, 3. Those who are living upon the earth when the intercession of Christ shall cease in the sanctuary above are to stand in the sight of a holy God without a mediator. Their robes must be spotless, their characters must be purified from sin by the blood of sprinkling. Through the grace of God and their own diligent effort they must be conquerors in the battle with evil. While the investigative judgment is going forward in heaven, while the sins of penitent believers are being removed from the sanctuary, there is to be a special work of purification, of putting away of sin, among God's people upon earth. This work is more clearly presented in the messages of Revelation 14.

True, this paragraph has occasioned much fear among Seventh-day Adventists because they have missed the Good News in it. In an effort to lessen the fear, some writers and teachers have tried to get around its obvious meaning by lowering the standard of being "spotless" and "purified." They contradict it by saying that one's *character* need not be either. All that is needed is a *legal* imputation of external righteousness.

Efforts are made to evade the problem by saying that the spotless Christ must continue to substitute for, and thus cover, our continued sinning. This must continue, they say, after "[His] intercession … shall cease in the sanctuary above." Again, this denies the statement, for it says the opposite. The 1888 message was "the beginning" of the answer to the problem:

(1) Christ's sacrifice on His cross secured a legal justification for "all men." It was then that He became our Substitute. Because their "trespasses" were all "imputed" unto Him, a "spotless" garment was thus *legally* accounted to "all men." They have received their present life only by virtue of His dying in their place. Thus "all men" have been "elected" to salvation.

All fear of being lost is annihilated by a heart-appreciation of His accomplishment on His cross. In the last hours of human history a people will at last "comprehend" what it means. As High Priest, Christ will accomplish everything He died to accomplish not only for His people but in them, *if we will stop hindering Him.*

(2) The above statement clearly says that it is Christ who "shall purify the sons of Levi, and purge them." It is His "blood of sprinkling" that purifies them. The cleansing of the sanctuary is not the work of the people; it is the work of the High Priest. It is due to His divine initiative; His people indeed have something to do, but their work is to *cooperate* with Him, to let Him do it (cf. Philippians 2:5; 3:15; Colossians 3:15, etc.).

(3) The cleansing of the sanctuary is the "final atonement," the fruition of all that Christ accomplished on His cross. He is the "Saviour of the world." We are not anybody's saviour, least of all our own.

But wait a minute! The statement says it is by "their own diligent effort [that] they must be conquerors." My lack of "diligent effort" is what makes me afraid.

Read it again. It says, *"through the grace of God and their own diligent effort ..."* Which comes first?

Again the thought is clear that the High Priest will do this work *if we don't hinder Him.* Our own "diligent effort" is the same as the "constraint" of *agape* which motivated Paul to live unto Christ and not unto self. "The love of Christ" imparts a new "under grace" motivation that takes the place of the "under the law" motivation imposed by fear. Our "own diligent effort" is never the work of our own initiative; it is always a response to the initiative of the Holy Spirit, the Comforter who is called to abide with us forever.

The thought of our robes being "spotless" should not paralyze us with fear any more than a bride worries about her wedding dress being "spotless" for her bridegroom to see. What motivates her is solely her love and respect for him, not fear that he will reject her. The reason why the Lord sent the 1888 message was that it might arouse in His people a concern for Christ like that of a bride for her husband. It is a totally different idea than the usual childish concern for our own personal security. In such "union with Christ," self-centeredness shrivels into the nothingness it is.

But how could such a "union" purify us from sin?

Because deliverance from self-concern through union with Christ always purifies from sin. The result that the 1888 message would have accomplished (had it not been hindered!) is set forth in Revelation 19:7, 8:

> Let us be glad and rejoice, and give honour to him: for the marriage of the Lamb is come, and his wife hath made herself ready. And to her was granted that she should be arrayed in fine linen, clean and white: for the fine linen is the righteousness of saints.

There is the "robe" that is "spotless." And "blood" has done the cleansing, because the Bridegroom is the Lamb who was slain.

But none of the ransomed ever knew
How deep were the waters crossed;
Nor how dark was the night the Lord passed through
Ere He found His sheep that was lost.
—*Elizabeth C. Clephane*

Ah, but at last there is a people who have learned to *appreciate* how deep were those waters crossed, how dark was the night that the Lamb went through! "The blood of sprinkling" is the essential element of the often-feared "investigative judgment." How tragic that the bride has held back for over a century, resisting our Lord "in His office work," to borrow Ellen White's phrase (*Review and Herald*, January 21, 1890). How doubly tragic that we have been fearful of the most blessed ministry ever achieved for us!

Imagine a woman's true lover seeking to woo her heart to surrender. But while she endlessly worries about spots on her wedding dress, she resists him and delays the wedding because she cannot understand or appreciate how much the bridegroom-to-be actually loves her.

Do you mean to say then that sin doesn't matter? That we don't have a lot of work to do in order to overcome?

Of course sin matters, and we do have a lot of work to do. The 1888 message simply says that the true glory of God is revealed in the blinding light of the cross. And sin cannot exist in that light. "Faith works by love and purifies the soul."

It is not we who purify the soul; it is faith which does the work. Over and over the dear Lord has tried to impress upon His people the 1888 truth that righteousness is by faith, not by works. It is not by *doing* that we wash our robes, but by *believing* in that blood of the Lamb.

And that is not cheap grace. It is terribly expensive grace. Only in the last hours of time do God's people at last learn to sense how expensive it is. And sin is forever vanquished because self-love is vanquished, and the great controversy is finally closed.

Yes, we have a lot of work to do: "This is the work of God, that ye believe on him whom he hath sent" (John 6:29). Our endless "work" is to learn what it means to believe!

It's impossible for any believing soul to go on in transgression of the law of God if he or she has a heart that, however cold and hard, has been melted by the sight of that "blood."

But how can one learn to "delight" in the law of God, the Ten Commandments?

What teaches us to say "No!" to ungodly lusts and all the compulsive addictions and perversions the devil can throw at us is not fear of punishment or hope of reward, but seeing that wondrous cross. The grace of God has actually brought salvation to all men, and it teaches us how to say that word "No" (see Titus 2:11, *New International Version*).

Like an ugly chrysalis metamorphosing into a beautiful butterfly, the Ten Commandments cease to be ten prohibitions, and become ten glorious promises. The Lord says in effect that if we will but appreciate what it cost Him to redeem us, how He has brought us out of the land of Egypt, out of the house of bondage, He promises that we will never steal, lie, commit adultery, etc. (see Ellen G. White, *Seventh-day Adventist Bible Commentary*, vol. 1, page 1105). This is because the Holy Spirit becomes a stronger motivation to the believer than the promptings of his sinful nature (cf. Galatians 5:16-18).

Do we as a church need the blessings of the 1888 message? "The Lord in His great mercy" sent it to us. Isn't it being rather arrogant to say that we don't need what the Lord sends us? What can Heaven think of us for neglecting it?

How does the 1888 idea of justification by faith, solve the problem of so many Adventists who lack "assurance of salvation"?

The truth of justification by faith in the 1888 message is the missing ingredient in both "historic Adventism" and the "new theology." Both generally follow the Arminian view, which in effect makes the sinner's salvation dependent on his own initiative.

This raises the question whether the believer can ever have a true assurance of salvation. Can he ever be totally sure that his cooperation or response has been sufficiently complete?

In contrast, assurance is locked in with the 1888 view. It recognizes that the sacrifice of Christ actually purchased justification for "all men." All that the human race is "in Adam" has been totally reversed by all that the human race is "in Christ." "God so loved the *world* that he gave his only begotten Son" (John 3:16). He tasted death (the second death) for "every man" (Hebrews 2:9). He is the propitiation for the sins of the believers, yes, but also for the "sins of the whole world" (1 John 2:2). No one is left out!

29

He is "the Saviour of all men, specially of those that believe" (1 Timothy 4:10). He has borne and still bears the true guilt of "all men," for "Christ died for all" (2 Corinthians 5:14, 15). Otherwise, "all" would already be "dead." This is a legal or forensic justification *effected*, not merely *offered as provisional*, for "all men."

Thus this gift is actually given to them "freely by His grace" (Romans 3:23, 24). Nothing can be a gift until it is given. "All men's" physical life, their next breath, all they have, they enjoy solely by the grace of Christ. And yet they may never have realized the true Source of the "grace of life" which they have had. Christ is so generous and magnanimous that He freely lets His sun rise on the good and on the evil, and sends rain on the just and on the unjust. In the same way He has encircled the world with an atmosphere of grace as real as the air we breathe (*Steps to Christ*, page 68).

Believe *that* Good News, and your alienation from God is healed. Paul makes clear that we cannot be worried about assurance of salvation if we see the cross: "He that spared not his own Son, but delivered him up for us all, how shall he not with him also freely give us all things?" (Romans 8:32).

I have been told to beware of this Good News, for there is danger of Universalism in it.

This is not Universalism—far from it. Some people will be lost, not because God has predestined them to be lost, but because they choose to resist, reject, and despise this grace, and refuse to "breathe" it. Calvinism's "irresistible grace" is not Biblical. "The sinner may resist this love, may refuse to be drawn to Christ; but if he does not resist, he will" be drawn all the way to repentance (*Steps to Christ*, page 26). But if he does resist, he takes back on himself at last the full condemnation from which Christ has already saved him (John 3:16-18). Thus in the end his damnation is due solely to his own initiative (see *The Great Controversy*, page 543).

How would you answer the objection of those who say this view lessens true obedience and strict adherence to high standards?

This is the precise objection that many of our dear opposing brethren raised at the 1888 Session. They initially rejected this "most precious message" because they were afraid that if our people fully appreciated how "grace did much more abound," they would become lax in keeping the law.

But Paul could have calmed their fears: "Do we then make void the law through faith? God forbid: yea, we establish the law" (Romans 3:31). *There is no other way to obey truly than by such genuine faith.* The superficial "only believism," or "cheap grace," of popular Christianity is not genuine faith. It does not understand the tremendous spiritual dynamite implicit in true justification by faith.

The reason is because popular Christianity generally believes in the natural immortality of the soul. If that doctrine is true, Christ could not have truly died on His cross. Thus many cannot appreciate the grand dimensions of the *agape* revealed there. Like a row of dominoes falling, certain results are inescapable. Consequently, their concept of faith falls short; and in turn, their devitalized faith cannot "work" to produce full obedience to all the commandments of God. The result is worldliness, pride, self-sufficiency, and continued disregard of the law of God.

This is the reason why so many have declined obedience to the fourth commandment. It involves bearing a cross, and they don't know how to accept their own cross because they do not truly understand or appreciate Christ's cross.

In the final test of the "mark of the beast," all motivation to obedience which is based on either fear of being lost or hope of personal reward will prove to be self-centered. It will be "wood, hay, stubble" to be "revealed by fire" (cf. 1 Corinthians 3:12, 13). To change the metaphor, it will prove to be chaff blown away by the storm of the last days. The true "third angel's message in verity" prepares a people for that test of fire and storm.

But there are many sincere, honest people in all religions, waiting only to hear "the third angel's message in verity," and they will respond gladly.

Someone told me that the 1888 message teaches that the sinful human race was made righteous against and without their will, that the heathen and Satan worshippers, murderers and thieves, are all righteous. Is this true?

This is a distortion of the message. It says nothing remotely like this. Paul also had to contend with those who distorted his message.

The view of the 1888 messengers whom Ellen White supported is as follows:

As the condemnation came upon all [Romans 5:18], so the justification comes upon all. Christ has tasted death for every man. Hebrews 2:9. He has given Himself for all. Nay, He has given Himself to every man. The free gift has come upon all. The fact that it is a free gift is evidence that there is no exception. If it came upon only those who have some special qualification, then it would not be a free gift. It is a fact, therefore, plainly stated in the Bible, that the gift of righteousness [justification] and life in Christ has come to every man on earth (E. J. Waggoner, *Signs of the Times*, March 12, 1896; *Romans: The Greatest Treatise Ever Written*, page 104, CFI ed., 2019).

This is in harmony with John 3:16, 17; Romans 3:23, 24; 5:12-18; 1 Timothy 2:6; 4:10; 2 Timothy 1:10; Hebrews 2:9; 1 John 2:2.

But this is not *justification by faith*. It is purely a legal, "temporary" or "corporate" justification. But this does not make anyone to be experientially righteous unless and until he believes. It is the foundation on which justification by faith rests.

It is clear that the Bible teaches this beautiful truth. But does Ellen White agree?

Ellen White never disagrees with the Bible. But we sometimes read her with a veil of unbelief over our eyes in the same way the ancient Jews read the Old Testament, failing to see justification by faith therein.

We find Ellen White repeatedly recognizing this truth. For example, consider *Our High Calling*, page 52: "The mediatorial work of Christ commenced with the commencement of human guilt and suffering and misery, as soon as man became a transgressor." The word "man" means "all men," and Christ's work for us "commenced" before we repented. Also consider *The Desire of Ages*, page 660:

To the death of Christ we owe even this earthly life. The bread we eat [who is the "we"?—"all men"] is the purchase of His broken body. The water we drink is bought by His spilled blood. Never one, saint or sinner, eats his daily food, but he is nourished by the body and the blood of Christ. The cross of Calvary is stamped on every loaf.

Shortly before Ellen White wrote those famous words, she commented even more forcefully in an unpublished manuscript on the reality of a universal legal justification:

All blessings must come through a Mediator. Now every member of the human family is given wholly into the hands of Christ, and whatever we possess—whether it is the gift of money, of houses, of lands, of reasoning powers, of physical strength, of intellectual talents—in this present life, and the blessings of the future life, are placed in our possession as God's treasures to be faithfully expended for the benefit of man. Every gift is stamped with the cross and bears the image and superscription of Jesus Christ. All things come of God. From the smallest benefits up to the largest blessings, all flow through the one Channel—a superhuman mediation sprinkled with the blood that is of value beyond estimate because it was the life of God in His Son (MS 36, 1890; *The Ellen G. White 1888 Materials*, page 814).

And consider *Selected Messages*, book 1, page 343: "He took in His grasp the world over which Satan claimed to preside as his lawful territory, and by His wonderful work in giving His life, He restored *the whole race of men to favor with God*" (emphasis supplied).

Again: "Jesus, the world's Redeemer, stands between Satan and every soul. ... The sins of everyone who has lived upon the earth were laid upon Christ, testifying to the fact that no one need be a loser in the conflict with Satan" (*Review and Herald*, May 23, 1899). "All the judgments upon men, prior to the close of probation, have been mingled with mercy. The pleading blood of Christ has shielded the sinner from receiving the full measure of his guilt" (*The Great Controversy*, page 629). Ellen White says that Paul's opponents who came to Antioch from Jerusalem refused to believe that Christ died for "the whole world" and thus legally justified "all men" (see *Sketches From the Life of Paul*, page 121).

"All men" would die in a moment if they had to bear the true guilt of their sins. So would Adam and Eve have died in the Garden of Eden had not a Lamb been slain for them "from the foundation of the world" (Revelation 13:8). This is what Paul means when he says that "the free gift came upon all men unto justification of life" (Romans 5:18). Ellen White believed it.

Can anyone be justified without obedience?

No sinner can be justified *by faith* without repentance and obedience; nor can he retain the experience of justification *by faith* without continued cooperation with the Holy Spirit, which is obedience.

If the unbeliever chooses to reject what Christ has already done for him and thrusts it from him, he takes the full burden of guilt back upon himself and must die the second death. But that is totally unnecessary except for his stubborn unbelief.

This is the 1888 idea of justification by faith. It upholds the law of God as nothing else can do. Writing under the blessing of the 1888 message, the Lord's servant cleared up the problem of "conditions":

> The question will come up, How is it? Is it by conditions that we receive salvation? Never by conditions do we come to Christ. And if we come to Christ, what is the condition? The condition is that by living faith we lay hold wholly and entirely upon the merits of the blood of a crucified and risen Saviour. When we do that, then we work the works of righteousness. But when God is calling the sinner in our world, and inviting him, there is no condition there; he is drawn by the invitation of Christ and it is not, "Now you have got to respond in order to come to God." The sinner comes, and as he comes and views Christ elevated upon that cross of Calvary, which God impresses upon his mind, there is a love beyond anything that is imagined that he has taken hold of. … Christ is drawing everyone that is not past the boundary (MS 9, 1890).

Is there a conflict between the apostle James and the apostle Paul over righteousness by faith? Does James weaken Paul's gospel?

James (chapter 2:17-25) is not trying to contradict Paul. His point is that there are two kinds of faith—living and dead. There are also two kinds of people—living and dead. The dead people don't work, and dead faith doesn't work.

The kind of faith which the devils have when they "tremble" is a dead faith which does not appreciate the *agape* of Christ, and it does not produce works of righteousness. Paul is talking about a living faith which does appreciate the cross and moves us to willing and joyful obedience (Romans 13:10; Galatians 5:5, 6; 2 Corinthians 5:14-6:1).

The Jews said unto Jesus, "What shall we do, that we might work the works of God?" Just the thing that we want to know. Mark the reply: "This is the work of God, that ye believe on Him whom He hath sent" (John 6:28, 29). Would that these words might be written in letters of gold and kept continually before the eyes of every struggling Christian. The seeming paradox is cleared up. Works are necessary; yet faith is all-sufficient, because faith does the work. ...

The trouble is that many people in general have a faulty conception of faith. ... Faith and disobedience are incompatible. No matter how much the law-breaker professes faith, the fact that he is a law-breaker shows that he has no faith. ... Let no one decry faith as of little moment.

But does not the apostle James say that faith alone cannot save a man, and that faith without works is dead? [Waggoner asks this question.]

Let us look at his words a moment. Too many have with honest intent perverted them to a dead legalism. ... If faith without works is dead, the absence of works shows the absence of faith; for that which is dead has no existence. If a man has faith, works will necessarily appear. ...

Then how about James 2:14, which says: "What doth it profit, my brethren, though a man say he hath faith, and have not works? can faith save him?" [Waggoner also asks this question.]

The answer necessarily implied is, of course, that it cannot. Why not?—Because he hasn't it. What doth it profit if a man say he has faith, if by his wicked course he shows that he has none? Must we decry the power of faith simply because it does nothing for the man who makes a false profession of it? ... Faith has no power to save a man who does not possess it (E. J. Waggoner, *Bible Echo*, August 1, 1890).

While it is true that James does not contradict Paul, people have tried to make him do so. His perspective is different. He never once mentions the cross or the blood of Christ. Somehow the Holy Spirit saw fit to let us have 14 letters from Paul in our New Testament, and only one from James.

NOTES

2

PRACTICAL QUESTIONS ABOUT THE 1888 MESSAGE

Does the 1888 message do something practical for those who believe it?

Yes, it worked revival and reformation among the lay members who heard it immediately after the Minneapolis Conference (see A. V. Olson, *Through Crisis to Victory*, pages 56-81). The reformation would have been complete had it not been for the continued opposition of General Conference and *Review and Herald* leaders (Ellen White, *Review and Herald*, March 11, 18, 1890). The message brings joy and hope to thousands of hearts today who hear and believe.

How does temperance and health reform relate to the 1888 message?

The 1888 message recovers the true motivation for temperance and health reform by relating justification by faith to the cleansing of the heavenly sanctuary.

Although we are living in the antitypical Day of Atonement there is a current general disregard of this truth within the church. Meanwhile, so-called "moderate drinking" has become such a problem that articles are now appearing in our official church press seeking to meet the problem.

Biblical prohibitions of alcohol were generally taught by the Evangelical churches prior to National Repeal in 1933, but Evangelicals have now largely abandoned those once-held convictions in favor of so-called "moderate drinking."

Why have Evangelicals largely lost their anti-alcohol zeal?

They have lacked the motivation that understanding the Day of Atonement truth would provide. We too may cite the same Biblical prohibitions, "don't drink," "say 'no,'" etc., but without that grand motivation of the sanctuary truth they will prove equally ineffectual among us, especially among our youth. There is at present an alarming increase of social drinking in some Adventist circles.

The unique sanctuary truth is the hub from which have radiated all the spokes of Adventist health and temperance reform. Its neglect appears related to our drinking problem.

Why is righteousness by faith in the Day of Atonement setting so important?

Ellen White says that "the correct understanding of the ministration in the heavenly sanctuary is the foundation of our faith" (*Evangelism*, page 221), "the central pillar that sustains the structure of our position at the present time" (Letter 126, 1897). Unless we understand it clearly, "it will be impossible … to exercise the faith which is essential at this time" (*The Great Controversy*, page 488). The only true deterrent to intemperance is that "faith." Fear of sickness or accidents, even of death and hell itself, is not a strong enough motivation. We can drum away with the fear motivation endlessly, but it will not hold our youth in times of temptation:

> We may dwell upon the punishing of every sin, and the awfulness of the punishment inflicted on the guilty, but this will not melt and subdue the soul (MS 55, 1890).

Did Israelites in ancient times drink alcohol?

While it is very true that God has always prohibited use of alcohol, His people in ancient times did have a problem with it. (See, for example, Genesis 9:20, 21; 1 Samuel 25:36-38; Ruth 3:7; 2 Samuel 13:28, etc. The Bible has also prohibited worldliness and materialism, but both were practiced.) *But the people of Israel never took a drop on the Day of Atonement* (Leviticus 16:29, 30; 23:27-32).

It is true that intemperance and "moderate drinking," even drug usage, "abound" today, even within the church. But nothing can solve this problem except a revelation of "much more abounding grace," the kind that is ministered by the great High Priest in His closing work of atonement in the Most Holy Apartment.

In these "perilous" last days a better motivation must be found than self-concern or even us-concern, and that is concern for the honor and vindication of the One who gave Himself for us. Speaking again of the 1888 message, Ellen White related it to the Day of Atonement truths:

We are in the day of atonement, and we are to work in harmony with Christ's work of cleansing the sanctuary from the sins of the people. … We must now set before the people [that includes our youth] the work which by faith we see our great High-priest accomplishing in the heavenly sanctuary (*Review and Herald*, January 21, 1890).

What is the truly effective motivation for temperance and health reform?

The true reason for practicing health reform in general is not so we can enjoy a few more years of life in order to pursue ease and luxury, but that we may have clearer minds to comprehend the work of Christ as High Priest in the final atonement. The increased health we enjoy is so we can serve Him and our fellow-men effectively, not play more fun-and-games for ourselves. It is a heart-response to His love rather than a self-centered concern of "what's-in-it-for-me."

The February 25, 1982 special *Adventist Review* issue on temperance included a brief mention of the cleansing of the sanctuary as the real reason for our Seventh-day Adventist health and temperance message. It would be wonderful if more could be said so that truth could appear again in our official press.

What is sin? Can we define it as a broken relationship?

"Relationship" is a foggy, fuzzy word. A relationship can be either good or bad. The word does not appear in Scripture. Instead, sin is there defined as transgression of the law or hatred of it (*anomia*; 1 John 3:4). Sin is more than a broken relationship; it is rebellion against God.

The difference can be illustrated in the cross of Christ. As He suffered there in the darkness, He definitely experienced a "broken relationship," for He cried out, "My God, My God, why hast Thou forsaken Me?" Yet that broken relationship did not mean that Christ sinned. In His total loneliness, darkness, forsakenness, and hopelessness, He chose not to sin because He chose to believe. "God is *agape*" (1 John 4:8). Therefore *agape* can endure a broken relationship without sin. This proves that "a broken relationship" cannot be an adequate definition of sin.

The Bible articulates more clearly the true definitions of sin and faith than the word "relationship" can express. Confusion engendered by this word could be the cause of many people's lack of assurance. Arnold Wallenkampf comments thus:

The word *relationship* is often bandied around in today's conversations. It is used also in the area of religion, implying a saving connection with God. But relationship is no panacea. A person or organization—or almost anything for that matter—sustains a relationship in some way to anyone or anything else. ... All the three travelers who saw the unfortunate man who had been robbed and beaten on the Jericho road (see Luke 10:25-37) sustained a relationship to him. So the word relationship is not adequate to describe a person's saving connection with God.

A relationship per se with God guarantees no salvation. Satan himself sustains a relationship to God. Salvation results only from a *friendship* relationship, or soul-fellowship, with God. It was only the Samaritan's *friendship* relationship to the suffering traveler that saved the latter from death (*What Every Adventist Should Know About 1888*, page 86).

This idea of Christ dying for "all men" raises the question, "When is one's name enrolled in the book of life?"

In the Index to Ellen White's writing there are many references to those who are "listed in the book of life." But with two exceptions, they do not say when the name is written there.

Even these two exceptions are not very clear: (1) "When we become children of God, our names are written in the Lamb's book of life, and they remain there until the time of the investigative judgment" (Ellen G. White, *Seventh-day Adventist Bible Commentary*, vol. 7, page 987). (2) "The sinner, through repentance of his sins, faith in Christ, and obedience to the perfect law of God, has the righteousness of Christ imputed to him; it becomes his righteousness, and his name is recorded in the Lamb's book of life" (*Testimonies for the Church*, vol. 3, pages 371, 372).

When can a sinner repent and become "a child of God"?

In some cases, at a very early age. In the womb of his mother Elizabeth, the child John the Baptist responded to the Holy Spirit (Luke 1:44). In the womb of his mother, Jeremiah was called, sanctified, and ordained to be a prophet (Jeremiah 1:5). In some sense Christ has been the "Saviour of all men" even before they respond. Because of His love, "all men" are candidates for eternal life by virtue of His sacrifice.

His sacrifice actually provided life for all men (Romans 5:18). The book of life and the gift of life go together. God will "have all men to be saved, and to come unto the knowledge of the truth" (1 Timothy 2:4). Since Christ chose to "taste death for every man" (Hebrews 2:9), He has ordained life for "every man," the opposite of the death He tasted for them.

Surely the Lord wants everyone's name to be in the book of life, and those names will remain there unless by choosing darkness rather than light, they veto the "election" to eternal life which God has already chosen for them (John 3:16-19).

In our darkness of mind we do not realize His gracious election to salvation until the time comes when we hear about it, believe, and respond. At that time, so far as we are concerned, our names are enrolled in that book.

At what age can a child be told that his or her name is enrolled in the book of life?

We must never draw a circle to shut a child outside of the assurance of God's election to eternal life. In *The Desire of Ages* we read that Christ "did not refuse the simplest flower plucked by the hand of a child, and offered to Him in love. He accepted the offerings of children, and blessed the givers, inscribing their names in the book of life" (p. 564). Children only two or three years old can pluck a flower and give it to you in love.

Paul had an unusual idea in Hebrews 7:9 that may help us understand. Levi "paid tithes in Abraham. For he was yet in the loins of his father, when Melchisedec met him." In other words, God inscribed in His "book" that Levi was a tithe-payer before he was even conceived! "God ... calleth those things which be not as though they were" (Romans 4:17).

Paul's illustration of the carefree child in Galatians 4:1 is also helpful. The son of the lord of the estate is being rudely bossed about by the slaves until he comes of age. At that time the boy does not realize who he actually is. But all the while, he is the true lord of the estate. His father had him "enrolled" as such before he realized it.

How is this truth important in soul-winning?

We are not to tell anyone that God plans to exclude him from heaven. The plan of salvation does not require the sinner taking the first step in His plan of salvation, for God has already taken that step "in Christ." And John 3:16 tells us that the sinner's part is to respond in heartfelt faith, for "with the heart man believeth unto righteousness" (Romans 10:10).

It is a part of the Good News to tell the sinner that God has predestined him to eternal life, for He has not predestined anyone to be lost. Thus in His infinite mind He has already considered the sinner as a candidate for heaven, and if he appreciates that great benefit and responds and overcomes, God wants to *retain* his name in that book of life. The sinner must understand that by continued resistance of God's grace he is taking the initiative to erase his own name.

If a patient's illness has been cured, he no longer needs the medicine. Do not our people today have a much better understanding of righteousness by faith than in past decades? Should not the 1888 message now be silenced?

A century ago Ellen White said of this message, "There is not one in one hundred who understands for himself the Bible truth on this subject [justification by faith] that is so necessary to our present and eternal welfare" (*Review and Herald*, September 3, 1889; quoted in A. G. Daniells, *Christ Our Righteousness*, page 87).

Do our people today enjoy a significantly better ratio of understanding? Daniells said in his day (1926) that he thought the answer was no, for he said that the 1888 "message has never been received, nor proclaimed, nor given free course as it should have been" (page 47). There are times when Evangelical concepts were imported and labeled as "the 1888 message," but its basic elements have been lacking. Motif analysis can document this fact. When in our present century of history can it be said that the 1888 truths were recovered and promulgated?

The *Adventist Review* of January 6, 1991, reported a current survey that 70 percent of our youth do not understand the gospel. By "gospel," the survey understands the basic Evangelical concepts as held by non-Adventist churches.

Therefore facts will very likely show that a much smaller percentage of our youth today understand the unique truths of justification by faith which Ellen White referred to above.

She would hardly have said that "not one in one hundred" in her day understood the popular Protestant concept of justification by faith as taught by Moody or Spurgeon, for they were well-known 19th-century preachers, and multitudes read their sermons. She referred directly to the 1888 message itself.

When these concepts are presented to our congregations today, many, youth and adults, frequently testify that they have never before understood them, even though they may have been baptized into the church years, sometimes even decades, before.

We do not have a prophet who can give us an inspired percentage figure now as was the case a century ago. Whether or not the ratio is better now than "one in one hundred," one fact is clear: if it were radically better, the church could not be lukewarm, because understanding and believing that glorious truth makes lukewarmness impossible.

I am trying to understand at what point justification becomes ours as an experience.

The only Biblical answer is—at the point that we begin to believe how good the Good News is. That is, at the point where our heart begins to appreciate what it cost the Son of God to redeem us. That is New Testament faith, and effective justification is by that faith.

According to Galatians 5:6, such faith begins to "work" immediately, and the experience is subjective justification by faith. E. J. Waggoner says our main problem is unbelief—the opposite of faith:

As to your being Christ's, you yourself can settle that. You have seen what He gave for you. Now the question is, Have you delivered yourself to Him? If you have, you may be sure that He has accepted you. If you are not His, it is solely because you have refused to deliver to Him that which He has bought. You are defrauding Him. ...

Now as to your believing His words, yet doubting if He accepts you, because you don't feel the witness in your heart, I still insist that you don't believe (*Christ and His Righteousness*, Glad Tidings ed., page 83; 1999).

Note that the objective justification has already taken place at the cross for "all men." Our sins were "imputed" unto Christ (2 Corinthians 5:19). But that objective justification makes no change in the heart. When the sinner appreciates this and believes, the subjective then becomes a reality—or at least it begins to be such. It continues and deepens all through life.

I'm still trying to understand what God requires before justification becomes ours in experience.

The only possible Bible answer remains one word: faith. That is all God asked from Abraham (Genesis 15:6). The Hebrew word "believe" is the root of our word "amen."

And Ellen White's answer is the same. The Lord asks for one thing: "If we come to Christ, then what is the condition? ... Living faith" (MS 9, 1890).

For example, note the Hebrew of Jeremiah 11:5—his response to the "covenant" the Lord spoke to him. Jeremiah made no word of promise such as Israel did at Sinai. He only spoke the word "amen." That is all that the Lord has ever required from any person at any time. A true response of faith includes within it a built-in dynamic—all the works and cooperation that make the believer fully obedient to all the commandments of God.

Does justification by faith take care of past sins only?

A mere confession of past entities of sin is not true confession in the sense of 1 John 1:9. We do not truly understand what our sins are in order to "confess" them until we realize that in fact our sins are deeper than we have superficially realized. "In Adam" the Bible sees the entire human race as one man. This describes our corporate relationship. If we did not have a Saviour, we would be guilty of the sins of the whole world—corporately. No one of us is innately, by nature, better than anyone else.

Romans 3:23 in the *The New English Bible* says that "all alike have sinned." Our true guilt is what we would do if we had the full opportunity such as others have had: "The books of heaven record the sins that would have been committed had there been opportunity" (Ellen G. White, *Seventh-day Adventist Bible Commentary*, vol. 5, page 1085).

According to the 1888 message, true justification by faith is an on-going present reality. Not only are there sins of the past, but there is buried sin of the present, heart-enmity against righteousness, that needs to be realized and then intelligently confessed.

Our personal guilt that we realize is for the sins that we know we have personally committed. But this is only the tip of the iceberg of reality, and shows us what the rest would be *but for the grace of Christ.*

The issue is not confessing so that "the past" will never confront us again. Even our true guilt of the present must not be left to confront us in the judgment. According to the above statement, the books of heaven record every sin that I *would commit* if I had "the opportunity." This must include the crucifixion of the Son of God! Therefore true repentance and confession must include this. And that brings us to Zechariah 12:10-13:1:

> I will pour out the spirit of grace and prayer on all the people of Jerusalem, and they will look on him they pierced, and mourn for him as for an only son, and grieve bitterly for him as for an oldest child who died. ... All of Israel will weep in profound sorrow. The whole nation will be bowed down with universal grief—king, prophet, priest, and people. ... At that time a Fountain will be opened to the people of Israel and Jerusalem, a Fountain to cleanse them from all their sins and uncleanness (*The Living Bible*).

A number of times Ellen White applies this passage to the sealing work that must take place before probation closes (cf. *The Desire of Ages*, page 300; *Signs of the Times*, January 28, 1903).

For many years "we" have misunderstood the 1888 truth of justification by faith. As a result, we have resisted the idea of corporate guilt and corporate repentance. There has been a famine for the righteousness by faith that truly cleanses the hearts of God's people (the King James Version says, "the house of David and the inhabitants of Jerusalem"). The Lord wants to grant to us this true realization; and then there will be that fountain opened for sin and for uncleanness. May that day come soon.

Is there not a danger of making the Good News too good?

The gospel is most certainly Good News. Not that the Lord saves us *in our sins* but *from our sins*. His job is being such a Saviour. And He is very capable. Our unwillingness to let the sin go is the problem.

It's not good news that He leaves us to wallow in sin while we cherish a vain hope. He does deliver from sin, and thus can prepare a people for His second coming.

We cannot be honest and deny that "God so loved *the world*, that He *gave* [not lent] His only begotten Son, that whosoever believeth in Him [not *does* everything just right] should not perish, but have everlasting life." His love is active; He is a Good Shepherd seeking His lost sheep. One has to resist His grace in order to be lost.

No, that Good News is pure, and it is good. It is good because the grace of God imparts to the believing heart a desire to relinquish sin. Then the believer is motivated to full obedience. Jesus says:

> Come unto me, all ye that labour, and are heavy laden, and I will give you rest. Take my yoke upon you, and learn of me; for I am meek and lowly in heart: and ye shall find rest unto your souls. For my yoke is easy, and my burden is light (Matthew 11:28-30).

> It is hard for thee to kick against the pricks (Acts 26:14).

I have heard that the 1888 message interprets some texts like this backwards from the way we have always understood.

Yes, that may be true. The pure gospel always upsets lukewarm church members. The usual understanding that has been drilled into our people, and especially our youth, is that it is very hard to be a good Christian, and very easy to be lost. Jesus says the opposite, as anyone can see who will consider His words of life.

Here is another text that is usually understood backwards:

> ... the flesh lusteth [strives] against the Spirit, and the Spirit against the flesh: and these are contrary the one to the other: so that ye cannot do the things that ye would (Galatians 5:17).

Most of us have thought this means that we cannot do the good things we would like to do. But the 1888 message does see it backwards from that! If we believe how good the Good News is, the Holy Spirit turns out to be stronger than the flesh, and since He is striving against the flesh, the flesh loses out, and we cannot do the evil things it would prompt us to do. In other words, this is a comment on Romans 1:16 where we read that "the gospel is the power of God unto salvation" (our word "dynamite" comes from the Greek for "power").

Light is stronger than darkness; love is stronger than hatred; grace is stronger than sin; and the Holy Spirit is stronger than the flesh. The 1888 view is correct, for verse 16 says: "Walk in the Spirit, and ye shall not fulfil the lust of the flesh."

Yes, the Bible may say that the Good News is very good; but doesn't Ellen White say it is not as good as that?

Ellen White never wants to contradict the Bible, and certainly not to contradict the Lord Jesus Christ. She does not deny the 1888 concept of justification by faith, but it is possible for us to read into her writings our own Arminian ideas that have been nurtured all our lives. Thus we can read her like the ancient Jews read the Old Testament—with a "veil" upon our heart (cf. 2 Corinthians 3:14-16).

When she talks about "retaining justification," the context always indicates she means *justification by faith*. Anyone who willfully continues in sin immediately negates his experience of justification by faith. If he continues in sin and counts "the blood of the covenant, wherewith he was sanctified, an unholy thing" (Hebrews 10:29), he has done despite unto the grace of God and taken back the full condemnation upon himself. But nevertheless Ellen White is enthusiastic about the fact that the sacrifice of Christ embraced the whole world.

This must mean that no *legal* debit stands against us in the books of heaven unless we reject that justification already effected for us and which has already "come upon" us, to borrow again the phraseology of Romans 5:18. Christ took away the written indictment against us, nailing it to His cross (cf. Colossians 2:13, 14).

It is possible to take words, phrases, clauses, sentences, from Ellen White and string them together to give the impression that she is denying what Jesus said about His yoke being "easy" and His burden "light." But in context she would never dare to contradict the Lord Jesus who bought her with his blood. She did say this:

Yet do not therefore conclude that the upward path is the hard and the downward road the easy way. All along the road that leads to death there are pains and penalties, there are sorrows and disappointments, there are warnings not to go on. God's love has made it hard for the heedless and headstrong to destroy themselves. ... And all the way up the steep road leading to eternal life are well-springs of joy to refresh the weary (*Thoughts From the Mount of Blessing*, pages 139, 140).

If this turns out to be true, the Good News is good. But how does the Holy Spirit strive so successfully against the flesh?

The Holy Spirit comes as a Comforter (*parakletos*). It means the One called to come and sit down beside us and never leave us (*para* as in parallel, and *kletos*, called). He will never forsake us unless we beat Him off (John 14:16-18; 16:7-13).

An example of how He works is in Isaiah 30:21: "Thine ears shall hear a word behind thee, saying, This is the way, walk ye in it, when ye turn to the right hand, and when ye turn to the left." As you consider your past life, you can see that when you have made mistakes, it has always been because you have not listened to that "word."

Our part is to listen to Him, to pay attention, to respond to Him, to let Him guide us. When he convicts us of sin, our part is to say, "Thank You Lord; I believe it and I gladly give it up." If our response is not positive, we are resisting Him, and that is the only way we can be lost.

Sin is a constant resistance of the Holy Spirit, turning away from Him, choosing our way rather than His. The point of the 1888 message is that God is much more desirous of our being saved than we have thought. It's the job of the great High Priest to cleanse His sanctuary, not our job; yet we are to cooperate with Him, to let Him do it.

I would like to know more about why it is easy to be saved, and hard to be lost. This is a new idea!

In 2 Corinthians Paul explains this grand truth for us. He has been pouring out his life in unlimited service for Christ, enduring "labours more abundant, ... in prisons more frequent, ... thrice was I beaten with rods, once was I stoned, thrice I suffered shipwreck," and on and on he details his persecutions (11:23-28). Why not retire, and let the younger men bear these burdens?

Paul says he can't stop. He is defending himself against the charge that he is "mad" (Conybeare), or "out of my senses" (Goodspeed), or "insane" (Taylor): "For the love (*agape*) of Christ constraineth us" (5:14).

Paul says he was not made of better stuff than we are made of. He has simply *seen something that we have not seen*—the true meaning of the cross of Christ.

To appreciate the grand dimensions of *agape* as revealed at the cross supplies the missing motivation to serve the Lord. All self-centered motivation based on fear or hope of reward is childish, like the flower girl at the wedding who cares only for the cake and ice cream. In that sense, she is "under the law" (cf. Romans 6:14). The bride has discovered a better motivation for coming to the wedding—she is concerned for the bridegroom and couldn't care less about the cake and ice cream. She is "under grace," under a new motivation imposed by a mature heart-felt appreciation for the character, personality, and person of the bridegroom.

This is not to say that Paul was forced against his will. He could have chosen to despise the cross, and trample upon the crucified Redeemer. But he chose to *believe the gospel.* He goes on to tell us why that love became such a powerful motivating force to him:

> ... we thus judge, that if one died for all, then were all dead [or, all would be dead if He had not died for them]: and that he died for all, that they which live should not henceforth live unto themselves, but unto him which died for them and rose again (2 Corinthians 5:14, 15).

What do those verses mean in modem language?

The love of Christ is such a powerful motivation that it becomes impossible for the person who believes the gospel to go on living for himself. He now feels that constraint which moves him to live for Christ. The power of *agape*-love is the reason why it's easy to be saved and hard to be lost—if one's heart simply will *believe* the Good News.

Can you explain why The New King James Version actually says it is "difficult" to be saved (Matthew 7:14)? Doesn't this contradict the 1888 message?

The New King James Version text does say: "Narrow is the gate and difficult is the way which leads to life, and there are few who find it." But the King James Version does not say "difficult."

The Greek word translated "difficult" is *thlibo,* which means "compressed," "squeezed," "hemmed in like a mountain gorge" (cf. W. E. Vine, *Expository Dictionary of New Testament Words,* pp. 101, 102). But it is easy to pass through a narrow gorge if you drop your baggage. "Our" baggage is the love of self.

The King James Version correctly says: "Strait is the gate, and narrow is the way, which leadeth unto life, and few there be that find it."

Yes, but dropping my baggage is what I find so difficult. It is not easy to give up self.

That is very true unless we have seen the cross of Jesus. Go to dark Gethsemane, kneel down beside Jesus as He sweats drops of blood in His agony of temptation and hear Him pray, "O my Father, if it be possible, let this cup pass from me: nevertheless, not as I will, but as thou wilt" (Matthew 26:39). When your heart enters into union with Him by faith, you will find it easy to drop your baggage of the love of self, because you will be "incorporate in Christ," at one with Him, appreciating what it cost Him to save you.

If we make the Good News too good, won't people take advantage of it and continue in sin?

No, because "the gospel is the power of God unto salvation" (Romans 1:16). *Nothing else can save us from sin!* The sinner is not moved by bad news or by fear, but by the revelation of God's love (cf. *The Desire of Ages*, page 480). It is "the goodness of God [that] leadeth thee to repentance" (Romans 2:4). Only a willful misunderstanding can misconstrue the gospel.

I have always somehow gained the impression that God is going to judge me and condemn me if I give Him even a chance to do so. Can the 1888 message give me some light at the end of my tunnel?

Heaven's grand machinery is geared especially for saving sinners, not for condemning them (John 3:17). Many people are surprised to learn that the Father has refused to judge anyone, but has turned all judgment over to the Son (John 5:22). The text says that He has washed His hands of all judgment, and put it in Christ's hands, because He is the Son of man. Therefore you can be certain that the Father will never condemn you.

You can be equally certain that Christ will not condemn you. He says that He refuses to judge anyone with condemnation. The only judgment He will pronounce is the vindication, the acquittal, of those who appreciate His cross: "If any man hear my words and believe not, I judge him not: for I came not to judge the world, but to save the world" (John 12:47).

Therefore anyone who is condemned at last will be condemned by his own self-incriminating judgment because he has chosen not to believe the gospel: "He that rejecteth Me, and receiveth not My words, hath one that judgeth him: the word that I have spoken, the same shall judge him in the last day" (vs. 48).

The "wrath" that the Lord wants to save us from is not "God's wrath," as some mistaken modern translations render Romans 5:9 (the original language says, "we shall be saved from wrath through Him"; cf. the *Good News Bible, New International Version,* and *Goodspeed,* which insert a phrase that is not in the original). God would save us from the terrible experience in the last judgment day of our own wrath, of hating ourselves for a lifetime of self-seeking, wasted opportunities, and totally unjustified rebellion against His grace.

It's all very well to say that it's easy to be saved, "if you believe the Good News." My problem is that I find it hard to believe.

This is a very practical question. We must agree that the most difficult thing we have to "do" is to believe. We have all been born, bred, trained, nurtured, and conditioned, in unbelief. We wake up every morning afresh as an unbeliever, and need to humble our hearts anew to choose to believe.

A thousand times a day we need to choose again to believe what the Lord says. "I die daily," says Paul (1 Corinthians 15:31). Israel could not "enter in" their Promised Land because of unbelief (Hebrews 3:12-19; 4:6), and that is our problem still today.

Our battle is always "the good fight of faith" (1 Timothy 6:12), in other words, learning how to believe!

How can I learn to believe?

We have been told by an inspired writer that we can never perish if we will learn to pray a certain simple prayer. We find it in Mark 9 where a distraught father of a demon-possessed child begged Jesus, "If thou canst do anything, have compassion on us, and help us." Jesus turned his "if" right around backwards, and said to him, "If thou canst believe, all things are possible to him that believeth."

It seemed almost that Jesus was tantalizing him, dangling a glorious blessing before him just out of his reach, as we so often feel. The man thought he simply could not believe. But then he burst into tears, cast himself at Jesus' feet and prayed this prayer: "Lord, I believe; help thou mine unbelief" (vss. 23, 24). "You can never perish while you do this— never" (*The Desire of Ages,* page 429).

"God hath dealt to every man the measure of faith" (Romans 12:3). In other words, the Lord has granted each of us the capability to believe. The word "measure" is *metron*, like a vessel for measuring a liquid. In other words, He has "dealt to every man" a capacity for believing. No one can accuse Him in the judgment day that He withheld that "measure."

No human being can possibly believe until first of all he hears the Good News. You cannot originate faith within yourself apart from understanding God's love. No one has a self-starter. We cannot make our own atonement apart from the revelation of Christ.

Even faith itself is the gift of God (Ephesians 2:8). "How then shall they call on him in whom they have not believed? and how shall they believe in him of whom they have not heard? and how shall they hear without a preacher … [of] glad tidings of good things! … Faith cometh by hearing, and hearing by the word of God" (Romans 10:14-17).

The moment you hear the smallest beginning of that Good News, make a choice immediately to believe it. Don't delay even a moment.

If it is easy to be saved, do we never have a battle to fight?

Yes, we do have a terrible battle to fight, but it is not where we have often supposed it is—with obedience and hard works that we don't know how to do. The real battle is with ingrained unbelief. It is what Paul calls "the good fight of faith" (1 Timothy 6:12).

Fight it! Get on your knees, wrestle your way through that maze of darkness to the light beyond. If it takes time to fight the battle, it is time well spent. If it takes hours, even days, of fasting and prayer, you will emerge a victor. The struggle is well worthwhile. And if you decline the struggle, you must always endure the conviction of your sin of unbelief.

I need help in fighting that battle!

You can get the precise help you need in the Bible. David had to fight the same battle over and over again. Read his Psalms. Make your choice to believe, even in what appears to be total darkness, and then you can say with him, "O Lord, truly I am thy servant, and the son of thine handmaid: thou hast loosed my bonds" (116:16). Then you will find your feet set on the solid rock, and you will have a song to sing for ever afterward (40:1-4).

But all this "battle" does not mean that it is harder to be saved than to be lost, or easier to be lost than it is to be saved. All the angels of heaven are on your side; the Holy Spirit is striving against your flesh; Christ as the Good Shepherd is seeking you and trying to bring you back to His fold again; you have constant evidences of His grace. All this is making it easy for you to be saved, if you will choose to believe.

But if you choose not to believe, you face a wearisome struggle to stifle the convictions of the Holy Spirit. This is His constant pleading not to crucify Christ afresh. *That is difficult for any honest heart to do!*

You need to grasp the truth that God as the Father, the Son, and the Holy Spirit, is your Friend, not your enemy. Even though you may have been in darkness all your life, begin thanking the Lord for light you can't yet see, for blessings you can't yet feel. If He "calleth those things which be not as though they were," it's time you begin to do the same through believing His word. The light is shining on you, for Christ is "the true Light, which lighteth every man that cometh into the world" (John 1:9).

In Bunyan's *Pilgrim's Progress* we read of Christian asking the way to the Celestial City. Evangelist, pointing, asks, "Do you see yonder wicket gate?" "No," says Christian. "Do you see yonder shining light?" Then he wisely replies in behalf of all of us natural-born unbelievers, "I *think* I do." Says the Evangelist, "Keep that in your eye, so shalt thou find the gate."

If you think you have difficulty seeing the shining light, for sure there is one place where it is not quite as dark as all the rest. "Keep that in your eye." You will see the Light.

You say that God is a Friend. This raises the question, "Does God kill?" Does the 1888 message comment on this?

We are not happy to get into contention over this. We do not preach about it, and try to avoid the question wherever possible. We emphatically do not believe that our heavenly Father is a cruel tyrant worse than Goebbels, Hitler and Stalin, sadistic and vengeful toward unfortunate people who have failed to prepare to enter the New Jerusalem.

But we have no sympathy with torturous attempts to explain away or contradict Scriptures that clearly say that sometimes the Lord has slain people in an executive, judicial sense. They were in total, hopeless rebellion against the plan of salvation, and a curse to other people.

God's character is *agape*, it always has been and it always will be. But that does not mean that there is no executive sentence of death divinely pronounced upon the finally unrepentant wicked. There must come a time when He withdraws His subsidized life-support system from them. The Bible speaks of God as doing what He does not prevent.

In such a judgment of doom God will not act unilaterally. It will be ratified by the entire universe (Revelation 16:5-7). For Him to withdraw His sustenance from the wicked is a "strange work" (Isaiah 28:21). But it is a further revelation of His love, for it would not be love to perpetuate the existence of people who would only be miserable in it.

The 1888 messengers emphasized God's character of love when they discussed the final fate of the lost:

> The work of the gospel being finished means only the destruction of all who then shall not have received the gospel (2 Thessalonians 1:7-10); for it is not the way of the Lord to continue men in life when the only possible use they will make of life is to heap up more misery for themselves (A. T. Jones, *The Consecrated Way*, Glad Tidings ed., page 119; 2003).

The unbeliever who rejects the Saviour "is condemned already, because he hath not believed in the name of the only begotten Son of God" (John 3:18). Now he lives under judgment.

When God is forced to withdraw that life-subsidy which the lost have repeatedly despised, they must perish. Actually, for the finally impenitent to face Him in judgment will be self-destruction, for "our God is a consuming fire" to sin (Hebrews 12:29). Therefore those who have clung to sin like a vine clings around a tree must of necessity perish with the sin itself.

Does Ellen White give us any help with this question?

She has made a number of statements which are in harmony. We cannot cite them all. Here are a few:

> "Whatsoever a man soweth, that shall he also reap" Gal. 6:7. God destroys no man. Every man who is destroyed will destroy himself. When a man stifles the admonitions of conscience, he sows the seeds of unbelief and these produce a sure harvest (*Our High Calling*, page 26).

> God does not stand toward the sinner as an executioner of the sentence against transgression; but He leaves the rejectors of His mercy to themselves, to reap that which they have sown (*The Great Controversy*, page 36).

God has declared that sin must be destroyed as an evil ruinous to the universe. Those who cling to sin will perish in its destruction (*Christ's Object Lessons*, page 123).

How will that reaping or "destruction" take place? Ellen White does not contradict herself. The following resolves all apparent contradiction and demonstrates that there is perfect harmony with her many other statements:

Christ says, "All they that hate Me love death." God gives them existence for a time that they may develop their character and reveal their principles. This accomplished, they receive the results of their own choice. By a life of rebellion, Satan and all who unite with him place themselves so out of harmony with God that His very presence is to them a consuming fire. The glory of Him who is love will destroy them (*The Desire of Ages*, page 764).

Then does God actually kill the wicked in the last day?

Paul says that "the wages of sin is death" (Romans 6:23), and the version that says "sin pays its own wages—death," is not inaccurate. If one smokes cigarettes for many years and dies of lung cancer, can we say that God has destroyed him? In a sense He has, for it is His laws that the smoker has transgressed. But the smoker has surely destroyed himself, according to all understanding of human language.

Controversy and anathemas over this issue are out of place. Let us not split churches and alienate brethren and sisters. One can read ten texts in Scripture that say that God hardened Pharaoh's heart; and there are ten texts that say he hardened his own heart (cf. Exodus 8:15, 32 and 9:12, etc.).

If we find ourselves getting angry over this or other debatable points, we may end up being killers ourselves, for "whosoever hateth his brother is a murderer" (1 John 3:15).

How does repentance fit in with justification?

The goodness of God is already leading every human soul to repentance (Romans 2:4). It is a happy gift of God (Acts 5:31). Since it is sin that brings unhappiness, misery, and vain regrets, turning away from that sin automatically brings happiness.

A child of God confesses all his known sin and rejoices in salvation by faith today; but then tomorrow he remembers a deeper level of sin that he did not know of today. This is evidence that the Comforter has come, for His first work is to convict of sin (John 16:8). Blessed work! If He did not point out the sin to us, we would at last perish with it. During this great Day of Atonement, the Holy Spirit continues that work.

"Where sin abounded, grace did much more abound." … Then when the Lord, by His law, has given us the knowledge of sin, at that very moment grace is much more abundant than the knowledge of sin.

Then there is no place for discouragement at the sight of sins, is there? … It is the Comforter that reproves! Then what are we to get out of the reproof of sin? [Congregation: "Comfort."] (A. T. Jones, *General Conference Bulletin*, February 27, 1893).

And this goes on for a lifetime. At any given moment there is a level of "thou knowest not" in the heart's experience. "At every advance step in Christian experience our repentance will deepen" (*Christ's Object Lessons*, page 160). This is the work on earth that parallels the cleansing of the sanctuary in heaven.

You say this is a "happy work." On the surface, doesn't it look like unending misery?

Discovering these "loose ends" of a lifetime of selfishness and sin is not to overwhelm us with discouragement. The closer we come to Christ, the more we experience repentance, but Christ also experienced repentance in our behalf. Repentance is reality, and reality is true peace and happiness for the soul.

The sins of others are seen to be our sins, but for His grace. Since Christ did not sin, yet experienced a repentance in behalf of the sins of the world, it must have been a corporate repentance that He experienced (cf. Ellen White, *General Conference Bulletin*, 1901, page 36). We have never truly confessed our sins until we realize that our true guilt, apart from the grace of Christ, is the sin of the world. We can never say of someone else that we are *naturally* better than he or she. Any goodness we may possess is entirely Christ's imputation.

What does forgiveness mean?

We have never truly appreciated forgiveness until we realize what it is for, and how deep it must go. A superficial realization of our sin results in superficial forgiveness, and that in turn means superficial happiness. It will fail us in our hour of deepest need.

The Greek word for forgiveness means the actual taking away of the sin. A truly forgiven person will immediately hate the sin that has been forgiven. The English word reminds us that forgiveness means there has to be a "giving for" that has borne the punishment of the sin.

So, let the Holy Spirit get on with His work. Don't stop Him or resist Him. He is called the Comforter because the knowledge of our sin is indeed comforting Good News; it means there is hope for us.

If you have a deadly cancer but do not know about it, you are doomed. But if a knowledgeable physician tells you the truth so that you can have immediate surgery in order to save your life, isn't that good news?

And remember that when the Comforter convicts you of sin, it is that you may learn to understand the heart-needs of others. The time will come when our prayers will be others-centered, even Christ-centered, rather than self-centered or us-centered. Then we will truly be able to pray "in Jesus' name."

Granted that it's easy to be saved. But is it not easy to lose our salvation? I find it hard to maintain a devotional program.

Justification is always "by faith," never an exception by works. Therefore justification by faith is not "difficult to retain," as some say, unless it is difficult to believe.

And sanctification is as much "by faith" as is justification. Some deny this; but however we translate the words of Jesus, they end up with the same meaning when He says that we "may receive forgiveness of sins, and inheritance among them which are sanctified by faith that is in me" (Acts 26:18).

Therefore, again the problem comes back to believing. "As ye have therefore received Christ Jesus the Lord, so walk ye in Him" (Colossians 2:6). How do we "receive" Him? By faith. How then are we to "walk" in Him forever after? Obviously, by faith.

But I have heard it often said that although Christ gets us started, we must keep on flying on our own, keeping up our speed or we will crash.

The legalists of the Galatian believers apparently believed that only initial justification was by faith, but then afterward they were to maintain the Christian life by good works. Paul set them straight: "Received ye the Spirit by the works of the law, or by the hearing of faith? Are ye so foolish? having begun in the Spirit, are ye now made perfect by the flesh?" (Galatians 3:2, 3).

Our salvation does not depend on our holding on tight to God's hand, but on our believing that He is holding on to our hand (Isaiah 41:10, 13).

I have been told that I must "read the Bible, pray, and witness," in order to retain salvation. These are the very things I find difficult to do.

It is good to read the Bible, pray, and witness, but doing these things as works is not the way to retain salvation. If it is true that God takes the initiative in our salvation, it is equally true that He maintains that initiative.

In other words, once you begin the Christian life, the Lord does not back off like a car salesman when you have bought your car, leaving you to struggle thereafter on your own. Struggling on our own discourages us and hardens the heart.

The Good Shepherd still takes the initiative in looking for His lost sheep. He still keeps knocking at the door of the heart. And "He who has begun a good work in you will complete it until the day of Jesus Christ" (Philippians 1:6, *The New King James Version* [NKJV]). Never are we to think that our divine Friend becomes indifferent toward us.

How did Jesus in His humanity maintain His closeness to His Father? He was human; He had only 24 hours a day as we have; He was busy as we are, and He needed sleep as we do. He gives us a surprising insight into His devotional life: *the Father maintained the initiative.* Speaking of His prayer and Bible study life, Jesus says in the prophecy:

> The Lord God has given Me
> The tongue of the learned,
> That I should know how to speak
> A word in season to him who is weary:

He wakens Me morning by morning,
He awakens My ear
To hear as the learned (Isaiah 50:4, NKJV).

His Father awoke Him morning by morning that He might listen and learn. The Lord promises nourishing food to all who "hunger and thirst after righteousness" (Matthew 5:6). Since there is only one kind of righteousness (by faith), what the Lord is saying is that a lifelong hunger for more and more righteousness by faith is *happiness*. You are hungry to learn more and more, and never satisfied with what you learned yesterday, any more than you are satisfied with the food you ate yesterday.

We don't eat our daily food because the Bible tells us to, or even because Ellen White tells us to; we eat because we are hungry. A starving but hungry refugee in Africa is better off than a millionaire who is so sick that he has no appetite.

Ministers of the gospel have a peculiar problem here. They are often easily satisfied with what they learned in college or in the theological seminary, or what they learned in studying for a sermon last week.

The Bible reveals a loving heavenly Father and Saviour and Holy Spirit eager to maintain connection with us. He continually invites us to come to "breakfast," but of course if we are not hungry, we won't go.

How can I get this hunger and thirst?

This is what the Lord gives to those who hear and believe the Good News. They want more, just as when you taste something delicious, you want more. They don't have to set their alarm clocks to wake up in time, or force themselves to read and pray as a "work."

It is easy for us to make a devotional life into a works program. Charles Wesley was right when he wrote his hymn, "Jesus, Lover of my soul" even though the Church of England divines of the day were outraged at the idea. The Lord is the divine Lover of your soul; He is seeking you, actually wooing you.

But note how Jesus responded to His Father's daily initiative to awaken Him "morning by morning" to "learn":

The Lord God has opened My ear;
And I was not rebellious,
Nor did I turn away (Isaiah 50:5, NKJV).

Oh, how often we have been "rebellious," and turned away from His knocking at our door in the mornings! Sometimes it is because we have stayed up to watch the late-late show on TV, so that we have deprived ourselves of proper rest and made ourselves deaf to His appeals. (There is a reason why Scripture says that the day begins at sunset!).

To awaken in our souls that hunger and thirst is the purpose of the 1888 message of Christ's righteousness. The gospel is the bread of life; and once you taste it, you will ever after want to "eat" without being forced to do so. What joy! Always to be hungry and thirsty for more. The world's amusements, the TV, sports, vain pursuits, shopping, all lose their appeal when you "taste" the gospel for what it is. Many are now testifying that that hunger has been aroused in their souls by hearing or reading the 1888 message truths.

Suppose you keep trying but don't get that "hunger"?

This is not to say there is never a time for force-feeding. A sick person must temporarily be fed intravenously. But that is not the healthy way to live. And we never find health by taking pills and capsules instead of wholesome food. Five or ten minutes of hurriedly forced Bible study and a casual prayer are not adequate spiritual nourishment.

If you get sick with the flu, don't you take a day off from school or work in order to stay in bed and recuperate? Why not take a day off for fasting and prayer? Not seeking the Lord as though He were trying to hide from you, but taking the time to listen to Him as He seeks you.

That's what Isaiah means when he says, "Seek ye the Lord while He may be found, call ye upon Him while He is near" (55:6). He is not hiding from you—He is "near." (The Hebrew word translated "seek" means inquire of, pay attention to; see 1 Samuel 28:7).

Begin with confidence that the Lord will keep His promise to you. He says that "He is a rewarder of them that diligently seek Him" (Hebrews 11:6). Again, your job is to believe Him!

I have a problem with "the third angel's message" in Revelation 14:9-11. It is supposed to be Good News of "righteousness by faith," but why does it seem to be such very bad news?

Yes, there is a "fire and brimstone" ferocity that seems to permeate the third angel's message of Revelation 14:9-11. Youth think they see a terror-inducing portrayal of hapless sinners writhing in unprecedented torment day and night. And to make matters worse, "the holy angels" and Jesus Himself seem to enjoy watching this unprecedented human agony.

And what is the primary fault of these people in agony, according to Ellen White? It appears that they merely get one day of worship mixed up for another. Can this be true? Here's what the third angel says:

> If any man worship the beast and his image, and receive his mark in his forehead, or in his hand, the same shall drink of the wine of the wrath of God, which is poured out without mixture into the cup of his indignation; and he shall be tormented with fire and brimstone in the presence of the holy angels, and in the presence of the Lamb: and the smoke of their torment ascendeth up for ever and ever: and they have no rest day nor night, who worship the beast and his image, and whosoever receiveth the mark of his name.

On the surface, this comes across to many people as an appeal to raw fear. There is not a word here about grace, no mention of the cross or the love of God; and even compassion seems totally excluded, for God's "wrath" is to be "poured out without mixture" of mercy.

And all this high heavenly dudgeon seems to be provoked by a mere matter of people observing one day instead of another!

The most difficult problem youth have with this passage is the picture they get of "holy angels" and Jesus apparently presiding over this torture session like sadistic Nazi warlords gloating over the torments of their victims. Even though we may piously and indignantly reject this impression, the fact remains that many people think they see it in the Bible text itself.

To those who see light in the 1888 message of much more abounding grace there comes an added problem: how could Ellen White characterize this apparently raw terrorism as the gospel? To her, "the third angel's message in verity" is "most precious" (*Review and Herald*, April 1, 1890). Because they fear the problem, many pastors have stopped altogether talking about "the third angel's message."

How does this third angel's message have anything to do with the gospel of righteousness by faith?

Can we find help in the Bible itself? Please note:

(1) The third angel brings no isolated message on his own. Two

angels have preceded him and he only "followed them." The first one sets the stage, "having the everlasting gospel to preach unto them that dwell on the earth." Therefore the Good News must be in the third angel's message as much as in the first angel's.

(2) "The seal of God" is pure gospel, and is the other side of the coin of "the mark of the beast." John links the seal of God in Revelation 7:1-4 with the three angels' messages of chapter 14, because both passages are concerned with finding and saving a group of people known as the "144,000." The prophet realizes that there is no way that such a group can be prepared to stand "without fault before the throne of God" unless that "everlasting gospel" of grace is finally understood and proclaimed in its fullness.

(3) The "mark of the beast" is not a calamity or crisis that God brings on the earth. We are not to think evil of Him! According to Revelation 13, it is the devil who brings it as the final outworking of rebellious human history. And Heaven is powerless to prevent it. None of the horrors that prophecy predicts are what God brings; He is warning us of what human history will inevitably lead to.

(4) The third angel's message tells the world that human rebellion must lead to this final end. In mercy, this message is to prepare a people to meet that crisis.

(5) But these people cannot be prepared without an unprecedented revelation of the full dimensions of the "everlasting gospel," for only that "gospel ... is the power of God unto salvation." If there is an ultimate human sin, there must also be an ultimate disclosure of grace in order to meet it. Therefore the true third angel's message is gospel, and nothing else.

What is implicit here is the clearest, most powerful presentation of the Good News that has ever lightened the earth, because it must perform a work of grace never before accomplished. Never has such a group of "144,000" been prepared for withstanding Satan's final thrust of temptation, and for translation without seeing death.

(6) Those hapless people in torment are not guilty of a trivial fault of merely mixing up a day of worship. The Sabbath-Sunday issue is the difference between loyalty to the true Christ or loyalty to His enemy who will masquerade as though he were Christ. He will minister a false and counterfeit "holy spirit."

The problem is not jealousy on the part of Christ. When people choose to be loyal to Satan they actually invite suffering and death on themselves and on others. If allowed to go on, sin would sabotage the entire universe and bring the cosmic civilization of heaven to ruin and chaos, as it has already done to large parts of this planet. Sin is rebellion against God and high treason against His government.

(7) Satan's rule will ruin the earth. It will favor the love of self with its attendant pride and arrogance. The seal of God is the sign of the cross, the experience of self being crucified with Christ through an appreciation of His love revealed there. The mark of the beast is the opposite, the badge of devotion to self-interest, a total instinctive heart-reaction against such love. It is the signal for the final collapse of any semblance of order or security on earth. We cannot now imagine the scenes of horror that the final "time of trouble" will bring.

(8) All who receive that "mark of the beast" must ultimately involve themselves in a re-crucifixion of Christ in the person of His saints. Thus on the one hand there will come together at the end of time the full revelation of humanity's sinful depravity, and on the other hand the full disclosure of God's loving justice of *agape*. The third angel's message defines the issue and catalyzes humanity into those two camps.

Obviously, it means far more than we have superficially assumed. This must be why Ellen White said:

> There are but few, even of those who claim to believe it, that comprehend the third angel's message, and yet this is the message for this time. ... Said my guide, "There is much light yet to shine forth from the law of God and the gospel of righteousness. This message understood in its true character, and proclaimed in the Spirit will lighten the earth with its glory" (MS 15, 1888).

But doesn't it still look like God is losing His temper in this message?

Let's take a closer look at the original language. It gives us a different picture than of God having a hot-tempered tantrum. Several Greek words are usually translated in such a way as to give this "mad" impression, but they give us Good News when properly understood:

(1) "The wrath of God" is *thumos*, a word which means "passion" more than ill temper. For example, *thumos* is used in the second angel's

message to describe the "wrath" of the "fornication" of Babylon. Does one usually think of fornication as an outburst of anger? No; it is an indulgence of uncontrolled passion.

Arndt and Gingrich translate verse 8, "Babylon has caused the nations to drink the wine of her passionate immorality." Babylon has made the nations drunk with the unrestrained passion of her spiritual adultery. Now the third angel "follows" this new development by saying that God cannot help experiencing the normal response—a passion of righteous jealousy. Christ died to redeem the people of the world, and now Babylon is ruining the world. This portrays God in a different light.

(2) God's cup of "indignation" is *orge*, from which we get "orgy." Again, the idea is not so much hot temper as the loosing or abandonment of restraint. It is not that God wants to even a score against these unfortunate sinners. He experiences a divine, loving, and totally righteous reaction to the evil of sin which produces pain and death in His once-perfect world. This ultimate judicial response to sin is as much an act of God's *agape* as was Christ's sacrifice for sin.

Now at last that divine response must erupt unrestrained, because the wicked have made their final decision in favor of sin and its tragic consequences. They seek to destroy His people, whose corporate body is the Bride of Christ.

(3) The lost being tormented "in the presence of the holy angels" and in the presence of Jesus is *enopion*, from *en*, in, and *ops*, the eye, literally, in their eye, or before their face. The idea is not that Heaven in any way enjoys seeing their torment, like Inquisitors relishing an *auto-da-fe*. The "torment" of those who receive the mark of the beast is *totally self-inflicted*.

In Revelation 6:16 the wicked ask to be shielded from looking at "the face of Him that sitteth on the throne." Now in chapter 14 the sight of that face ("before the eye of") is what causes "torment," not a craven fear of the pain of punishment like a slave fearing his master's lash. It is the acute condemnation of sensing at last the total reality of their guilt, in contrast to the total righteousness of the Lamb whom they have despised. Ellen White comments on how seeing the face of Jesus and hearing His voice will mean torment to the wicked:

The wicked pray to be buried beneath the rocks of the mountains rather than meet the face of Him whom they have despised and rejected.

That voice which penetrates the ear of the dead, they know. How often have its plaintive, tender tones called them to repentance. How often has it been heard in the touching entreaties of a friend, a brother, a Redeemer. To the rejecters of His grace no other could be so full of condemnation, so burdened with denunciation, as that voice which has so long pleaded: "Turn ye, turn ye from your evil ways; for why will ye die?" ... That voice awakens memories which they would fain blot out—warnings despised, invitations refused, privileges slighted. ... They vainly seek to hide from the divine majesty of His countenance, outshining the glory of the sun (*The Great Controversy*, pages 642, 667).

Rightly understood, "the third angel's message in verity" prepares the repentant sinner to stand alive "before the eye of," "in the presence of the holy angels, and in the presence of the Lamb," without fear or shame or guilt. That is the ultimate measure of its grace. A world church, yes, the world itself beyond, is waiting to hear that message in its fullness.

NOTES

QUESTIONS ABOUT CHRIST'S COMING IN THE FLESH

I hear it said that it doesn't matter what one believes about the nature of Christ. Is this true?

We will let one of the 1888 messengers answer this question. Ellet J. Waggoner makes it clear how necessary it is for us to see Christ as He truly is. These are the first words of the first book he published after the Minneapolis Conference, showing how prominent this idea was in his message:

> In the first verse of the third chapter of Hebrews we have an exhortation which comprehends all the injunctions given to the Christian. It is this: "Wherefore, holy brethren, partakers of the heavenly calling, consider the Apostle and High Priest of our profession, Christ Jesus." To do this as the Bible enjoins, to consider Christ continually and intelligently, just as He is, will transform one into a perfect Christian, for "by beholding we become changed" (*Christ and His Righteousness*, Glad Tidings ed., page 7; 1999).

In a few words, what was the view of the 1888 messengers on the human nature of Christ?

Both understood that Christ took upon His sinless nature the fallen, sinful nature of mankind. This was so that He might be tempted in all points like as we are, conquer Satan, condemn sin in the flesh, and "succor" and save us in temptation. Yet He did no sin (Hebrews 2:14-18; 4:15). There was never the slightest doubt about Christ's full divinity; that was never an issue.

Why was this view so essential to their message?

This view was essential to their message of righteousness by faith because it saw Christ as "a Saviour nigh at hand, and not afar off," as Ellen White characterized it. Their idea of the gospel was glorious Good News of a Saviour who can save from sin, and prepare a people for the coming of the Lord.

As they saw it, if Christ had taken only the sinless nature of Adam before the fall, He could be Adam's Saviour, but we fallen sons and daughters of Adam would lack the assurance that He can save *us from sin*.

But seeing clearly that Christ took our identical nature, was tempted in all points like we are yet without sin, we can hope to overcome, even as He overcame. Sin is no longer the all-prevailing monster who (as multitudes think) has successfully proven God to be wrong. This issue is essential to resolving the great controversy.

Both Jones and Waggoner understood that the great controversy cannot be resolved simply by Christ paying a legal debt and legally substituting for our continued sinning. His people must also overcome even as He overcame.

How did the 1888 messengers reply to the charge that this idea is "perfectionism"?

Waggoner answers this question as follows:

> Now, do not get a mistaken idea. Do not get the idea that you and I are ever going to be so good that we can live independently of the Lord; do not think that this body is going to be converted. If you do, you will get into grave trouble and gross sin. … When men get the idea that their flesh is sinless, and that all their impulses are from God, they are confounding their sinful flesh with the Spirit of God. They are substituting themselves for God, putting themselves in His place, which is the very essence of the papacy (E. J. Waggoner, *General Conference Bulletin*, 1901, page 146).

> This sinful, mortal body will struggle for the mastery as long as we are in the world, until Christ shall come, and make this corruptible body incorruptible, and this mortal immortal. But Christ has power over all flesh, and he demonstrated this when he came in the likeness of sinful flesh, and condemned

sin in the flesh; and so when we consciously live by the faith of Christ, when he is in us by his own life, living in us, he represses the sin, and we are masters, instead of the flesh being the master (ibid., page 223).

How did this view of the nature of Christ get translated into simple, practical godliness?

It gave the sinner hope that the great controversy between Christ and Satan could come to an end, that sin is indeed "condemned in the flesh," that God's people can overcome, that He can have a people who honor Him in these last days. The prevailing Roman Catholic and Protestant view assumed that as long as human beings have a sinful nature, they can never truly overcome sin. Yet we are constantly told not to sin. Thus a never-ending tension is set up in the soul that leads invariably either to discouragement and fear that we can never measure up, or to presumption that it's impossible to overcome and therefore sin is OK.

The 1888 view sees Christ as fighting our battle with the enemy head-on, not "exempt" from the real struggle as the other view insists. It was this that so rejoiced the soul of Ellen White when she first heard it. Jones expressed it thus:

> Conversion, then, you see, does not put new flesh upon the old spirit; but a new Spirit within the old flesh. It does not propose to bring new flesh to the old mind, but a new mind to the old flesh. Deliverance and victory are not gained by having the human nature taken away, but by receiving the divine nature to subdue and have dominion over the human,—not by the taking away of the sinful flesh, but by the sending in of the sinless Spirit to conquer and condemn sin in the flesh.
>
> The Scripture does not say, Let this *flesh* be upon you, which was also upon Christ; but it does say, "Let this *mind* be in you, which was also in Christ Jesus." Philippians 2:5.
>
> The Scripture does not say, Be ye transformed by the renewing of your *flesh*; but it does say, "Be ye transformed by the renewing of your *mind*." Romans 12:2. We shall be trans*lated* by the renewing of our flesh; but we must be trans*formed* by the renewing of our minds (*Lessons on Faith*, page 91).

Some say that the nature of Christ was not a part of the presentations at the General Conference Session of 1888 in Minneapolis. Is there evidence that proves this true or false?

There is evidence that it is not true:

(1) Waggoner presented this view in his *Signs of the Times* articles beginning January 21,1889. They were later published almost word for word as *Christ and His Righteousness* (Pacific Press, 1890). He could hardly have gotten home from Minnesota to Oakland, California, in time to have the January 21 article ready for publication unless he had written it at the time of the Minneapolis Conference or immediately after. L. E. Froom reports that in his interview with Waggoner's widow she informed him that she had taken his Minneapolis talks down in shorthand, transcribed them, and that they became the basis of those articles (cf. *Movement of Destiny*, pages 200, 201).

(2) In 1887 Waggoner wrote a reply to G. I. Butler's book *The Law in Galatians*, entitling it, *The Gospel in Galatians*. He did not publish it until shortly before the 1888 Conference, and gave a copy to each delegate. In it he clearly articulates this view of the nature of Christ (pages 60-64).

The fact that W. C. White did not include in his handwritten notes at Minneapolis any mention of this subject proves nothing. The notes are far from being complete.

(3) The question is really immaterial, because both Jones and Waggoner continued to teach this view throughout the decade following 1888 while Ellen White's continuing endorsements extended through 1896 and even into 1897.

Does the General Conference recognize that the 1888 view of the nature of Christ may possibly be true?

Since the Palmdale Conference of 1976 the General Conference has recognized that both views of the nature of Christ are acceptable in the church. General Conference personnel are on both sides of the issue. Some strongly oppose the 1888 view; others openly proclaim it. Neither side can deny the other side the liberty of proclaiming either view.

Thus the General Conference grants liberty to those who believe the 1888 view because there is a trust that the Holy Spirit will bring a resolution of our differences as we "press together" in this time so close to the end. There is some evidence that this coming together is already beginning.

Was Christ tempted from within as we are tempted? Or was He tempted only from without as the sinless Adam was tempted in the Garden?

Scripture says that He was "in all points tempted like as we are, yet without sin" (Hebrews 4:15). How are we tempted? Both from within and without. Frequently Jesus makes clear that He was tempted from within, even as we are (John 5:30; 6:38, and Matthew 26:39). It was necessary for Him to deny self, for He says that in order for Him to follow His Father's will, He must deny His own will. Thus He bore the cross all His life on earth.

But the sinless Adam was not so tempted. He knew no inner struggle to deny self, for in his innocent state he was naturally in harmony with God without the necessity of bearing the cross. He was tempted only from without.

In 1894 Ellen White published a little booklet, "Christ Tempted As We Are." On page 11 she specifically says that our strongest temptations come from within, and Christ was likewise so tempted. Confusion comes when our people think that temptation is the same as sin. Christ proved that it is possible to be tempted and yet not sin.

Some say that 1 John 4:2, 3 has nothing to do with the nature of Christ discussions, but that it refers only to ancient Gnosticism. How did the 1888 messengers understand John's warning?

Let us look at the text:

Hereby know ye the Spirit of God: Every spirit that confesseth that Jesus Christ is come in the flesh is of God: and every spirit that confesseth not that Jesus Christ is come in the flesh is not of God: and this is that spirit of antichrist, whereof ye have heard that it should come; and even now already is it in the world (King James Version).

Both Jones and Waggoner understood this warning from John to apply to the Roman Catholic doctrine of the nature of Christ and to the similar popular Protestant view that Christ took upon Himself only the sinless nature (or flesh) of Adam before the fall.

The dogma of the Immaculate Conception declares that when the Virgin Mary was conceived in the womb of her mother, a miracle exempted her from inheriting the fallen, sinful flesh or nature of mankind. Thus the genetic link was broken in her case so that she could not be "of the seed of David according to the flesh." In this way she could pass on to her Son a sinless nature or sinless flesh, different from that of all mankind. The Catholic evangelist Fulton Sheen says she must be "desolidarized" from the human race so Christ can also be separated from us. In the light of 1 John 4:1-3, does this ring some bells?

Why is their doctrine so important to Roman Catholicism?

We have seen that this dogma means that Mary's Son, Christ Jesus, also was "exempt" from the genetic inheritance of all mankind and took only sinless flesh or a sinless nature. The basic idea is rooted in the doctrine of "original sin" which understands that if a person has a sinful nature it is impossible for him or her not to sin.

A little thought will show how the idea logically justifies sin. If there is indeed a great controversy raging between Christ and Satan, this dogma is a vote in favor of the enemy of Christ. And that is precisely what John says—it is the insignia of antichrist. It discloses the essence of the issue in the great controversy between Christ and Satan, in which the "little horn" of Daniel 7 and 8 figures so prominently. Satan's primary contention is that human beings who by nature have sinful flesh cannot truly obey God's law (cf. *The Desire of Ages*, page 24).

A little thought will also show how this is the prominent issue in the great controversy.

What specifically did Jones and Waggoner say about 1 John 4:2, 3?

Here is what Jones said about the text we are discussing:

In the view of the Catholic Church and of the dogma of the immaculate conception, the nature of Mary was so "very different from the rest of mankind," so much "more sublime and glorious than that of all natures," … [that it was] infinitely beyond any real likeness or relationship to mankind. …

It therefore follows … that in his human nature the Lord Jesus is "very different" from mankind, … infinitely beyond any real likeness or relationship to us as we really are in this world. …

But ... the scripture says, "He is *not* far from every one of us." Acts 17:27. ... The Lord Jesus ... took our nature of flesh and blood just as it is. ... Having found that the papacy puts Christ as *far away* from men as possible, it will be well to know how near to men he really is [quotes Hebrews 1:4]. ...

To deny this, to deny that Jesus Christ came not simply in *flesh*, but in the flesh, the only flesh that there is in this world, *sinful* flesh,—to deny this is to deny Christ [quotes 1 John 4:2, 3, 6]. ... Therefore this is the spirit of antichrist.

This tract was published by the *Review and Herald* in 1894, entitled *The Immaculate Conception of the Blessed Virgin Mary* (pages 7, 12). Ellen White's most enthusiastic and comprehensive endorsements of Jones's message and ministry are dated 1894, 1895, and 1896 (see for example, *The Ellen G. White 1888 Materials*, pages 1240-1255). She often specifically supported Jones's, Waggoner's, and Prescott's presentations of the nature of Christ.

It is impossible to deny that the Catholic view of the nature of Christ contradicts Scripture and is the keystone of the great apostasy. Waggoner fully agreed with Jones:

Was Christ, that holy thing which was born of the Virgin Mary, born in sinful flesh? Did you ever hear of the Roman Catholic doctrine of the immaculate conception? And do you know what it is? Some of you possibly have supposed in hearing of it that it means that Jesus Christ was born sinless. That is not the Catholic dogma at all. The doctrine is that Mary, the mother of Jesus, was born sinless. Why?—Ostensibly to magnify Jesus; really the work of the devil to put a wide gulf between Jesus the Saviour of men, and the men whom He came to save, so that one could not pass over to the other (*General Conference Bulletin*, 1901, pages 404, 406).

Is there a relationship between this Roman Catholic dogma and the popular view of the Evangelical churches?

Jones and Waggoner both said yes, there is a relationship between the popular Protestant view of the nature of Christ and that of Romanism.

Theirs was not an extreme or unreasonable view. We all know that Sunday-keeping by Protestants is a doctrine inherited directly from the Roman Catholic Church (and paganism). Likewise, the widely prevalent doctrine of the natural immortality of the soul has the same origin. It is not surprising that the popular Evangelical view of righteousness by faith is also infiltrated by the Roman Catholic concept.

Waggoner comments as follows in reply to this question:

> We need to settle, every one of us, whether we are out of the church of Rome or not. … Do you not see that the idea that the flesh of Jesus was not like ours (because we know ours is sinful) necessarily involves the idea of the immaculate conception of the virgin Mary? …
>
> It is so strange that it takes us so long to come to the very simple ABC of the gospel (idem).

If 1 John 4:1-3 does relate to the Roman Catholic dogma, it must also apply equally to any teaching which denies that Christ in His incarnation took the fallen, sinful flesh of mankind. (John's word "flesh" is *sarx*, which in the New Testament always means the fallen, sinful flesh that all mankind possess).

Some of our prominent Adventist speakers have ridiculed the 1888 view of the nature of Christ, saying that it makes us the "laughingstock" of the Evangelical churches. Why would Ellen White endorse such a message if it deserves ridicule?

Ridicule is often more difficult to endure than outright persecution by force. The apostle Peter thought himself strong to endure opposition, yet readily withered and denied his Lord before the ridicule of a girl. But ridicule does not overthrow truth.

The 1888 view of the nature of Christ may be ridiculed by some Evangelicals, but so is the Sabbath truth, and the sanctuary doctrine that is the "foundation of our faith." We would be very unwise to abandon a truth simply because some opponents ridicule it.

As soon as she heard the 1888 message of the nature of Christ Ellen White was courageous and bold enough to stand firmly for what she recognized to be truth. Both she and A. G. Daniells have written that she had to stand at Minneapolis "almost alone." While she urges us all to be "careful, exceedingly careful" how we speak of the human nature of Christ, she unhesitatingly approved of the way Jones and Waggoner presented it.

In this as in all other issues, the important question to ask is, What does the Bible say?

Was the Jones-Waggoner view of the nature of Christ something new that they discovered?

According to Ellen White, they found it in the Bible. Whether they read it in other authors of past centuries we do not know. But Harry Johnson, a Methodist scholar at the University of London, found evidence that all through the centuries there have been a minority of scholars and reformers who believed that truth, often at the expense of suffering intense persecution for it. His doctoral dissertation was published under the title, *The Humanity of the Saviour* (Epworth Press, London, 1962).

Some of these whom Johnson cites were: Gregory of Nyssa (330-395 A.D.), Felix of Urgel (f. 792), Antoinette Bourignon (1616-1680), Peter Poiret (1646-1719), Christian Fende, Johann Konrad Dippel (1673-1734), Gottfried Menken (1768-1831), Hermann Friedrich Kohlburgge (1803-1875), Edward Irving (1792-1834), Erskine of Linlathen (1788-1870), and Johann Christian Konrad von Hofmann (1810-1917), and Karl Barth. There was another whom Johnson did not cite—J. Garnier, author of a two-volume set entitled *The True Christ and the False Christ* (London: George Allen, 1900). Garnier set forth the theological implications of the sinless-nature theory and demonstrated that it is the fulfillment of the apostle's warning in 1 John 4.

Mezgebe A. Berhe, a student at the Andrews University Theological Seminary, has cited others whom Johnson missed: Cyril of Alexandria, Origen, Gregory Nazianzan, St. Hilary, Victorinus Afer, Ambrose, Gregory Bishop of Elvira, and Anselm of Canterbury (*The Sinful Human Nature of Christ*, unpublished manuscript).

By no means did all of these scholars clearly articulate the full New Testament concept, any more than they fully understood the prophecies of Daniel and Revelation. But they did at times make statements that indicate a leaning in the direction of this truth.

But what about the present time? Do all Sunday-keeping Evangelicals, without exception, reject the view that Christ took our fallen, sinful flesh?

By no means. The facts are that some very thoughtful Evangelical scholars are coming more and more to the view of Jones and Waggoner, simply as the result of more careful Bible study. Harry Johnson says:

> The humanity of Jesus is being taken seriously. We can heartily agree with D. M. Baillie's remark: "It may safely be said that practically all schools of theological thought today take the humanity of our Lord more seriously than has ever been done before by Christian theologians" (page 201).

At the same time some Evangelical scholars are coming to recognize that natural immortality is not Bible truth.

In fact, Baillie uses almost the same words as Waggoner used in 1895 to describe the inadequacy of the sinless-nature theory, saying the church in previous ages

> … was continually haunted by a docetism which made [Christ's] human nature very different from ours and indeed largely explained away as a matter of *simulation* or *'seeming'* rather than reality (idem, emphasis supplied).

Said Waggoner of the usual view of Romans 8:3:

> There is a common idea that this means that Christ *simulated* sinful flesh; that He did not take upon Himself actual sinful flesh, but only what appeared to be such. But the Scriptures do not teach such a thing (*Romans: The Greatest Treatise Ever Written*, CFI ed., page 131; 2019; emphasis supplied).

What factors have led these modern scholars to come to this view on this subject?

The answer has to be: simple Bible study. The Bible is as clear on the nature of Christ as it is on the seventh-day Sabbath. In fact, all one has to do is to let the following Scriptures be free to have their say, without comment or contradiction: John 5:30; 6:38; Romans 8:3, 4; 15:3; Matthew 26:39; Ephesians 2:14, 15; Colossians 1:21, 22; Hebrews 2:9, 18; 4:15; Revelation 3:21, etc.

Some of these modern non-Adventist scholars who have come to virtually the same view as our 1888 messengers are: Andrew Bandstra, Oliva A. Blanchette, Dietrich Bonhoeffer, Vincent P. Branick, C. E. B. Cranfield, Oscar Cullman, James D. G. Dunn, Francis T. Fallon, Victor Paul Furnish, David G. George, Florence Morgan Gillman, Roy A. Harrisville, Jean Hering, Morna D. Hooker, Ernst Kasemann, Richard J. Lucien, Reinhold Niebuhr, Anders Nygren, Alfred Plummer, H. Ridderbos, John A. T. Robinson, Martin H. Scharlemann, J. Schneider, J. Weiss, Charles A. Scott, Robin Scroggs, Robert H. Smith, David Somerville, James S. Stewart, and Harold Weis (see Berhe, op. cit.).

Does this mean that this impressive array of scholars are clearly teaching the 1888 message?

No, it must be stressed that not all of these scholars consistently maintain the view held by the 1888 messengers. Often they show that they are wrestling with the concept; but Berhe has assembled statements from them that clearly show how an honest conscience has motivated them at times to recognize it. There are other 1888 concepts that apparently few if any of them have as yet come to see.

Are the Evangelical churches accepting the view of these scholars on the nature of Christ?

It must be stressed that in general the Evangelical churches do not teach what these scholars are coming to recognize. If the 1888 view deserves to be a "laughingstock," it would follow that the above cited scholars deserve the same ridicule. But it is clear that the direction in which many are moving is toward the same view that "the Lord in His great mercy sent" to us a century ago.

We have no reason to condemn this view for fear of our Sunday-keeping brethren. If we had the courage to proclaim this "message of Christ's righteousness," many Evangelicals would see and gladly accept it, and it could make the Sabbath truth easier for them to see. Perhaps we Seventh-day Adventists have been woefully behind the keen cutting edge of modern Biblical scholarship in this area.

For sure, there is a widespread hunger for "the third angel's message in verity." Will not the Holy Spirit will bless its proclamation?

You proclaim the 1888 idea about the nature of Christ. In view of the fact that there is strong opposition to it, is this not divisive?

The clear Bible statements, the Ellen White comments, and the actual words of the 1888 messengers themselves, are not divisive. The contention and divisiveness arise from those who condemn what is so clearly the heart of the actual 1888 message.

Others have a right to their own views and deserve the religious liberty to proclaim them as they wish. We do not seek to silence them; we have confidence that as the result of free and open discussion based on full information, the church can arrive at truth.

If that "most precious message" of 1888 is actually error and if Ellen White was naïve and mistaken to endorse it as she did, clear cogent reasons should be forthcoming from those who oppose it. But they should not seek to silence the message without refuting it with clear Bible evidence.

Isn't the nature of Christ a minor matter that should be laid aside for the sake of church unity?

The New Testament presents the nature of Christ as tremendously important, as can be seen by reading Matthew 1:23; Luke 1:35; John 5:30; 6:38; Matthew 26:39; Romans 1:3; 8:3, 4; Ephesians 2:15; Colossians 1:21, 22; Hebrews 2:9-18; 4:15; 1 John 4:1-3, etc.

Ellen White says that "the humanity of the Son of God is everything to us" (*The Youth's Instructor*, October 13, 1898). And the 1888 messengers regarded it as the keystone of their message.

Is it not disrespectful to Christ to say that He was tempted like we are? People are tempted to do terrible things!

The Bible says He was tempted "in all points" like we are (Hebrews 4:15). We know for example that He was tempted to take drugs, for no one was ever more tempted to relieve pain than He was on His cross, yet He refused a drug (Matthew 27:34). Temptation itself is not sin. The sin comes in yielding to temptation, and Christ never yielded.

If there is some sin that people are tempted to commit for which Christ was not tempted, in that respect the sinner can feel that he has no Saviour: "In that He Himself hath suffered being tempted, He is able to succor them that are tempted" (Hebrews 2:18). God "hath made Him to be sin for us, who knew no sin" (2 Corinthians 5:21). On the cross that terrible reality was fulfilled. On the cross He realized to the full the evil of human sin.

Writing to a youth who was tempted as all youth are tempted, Ellen White said: "I present before you the great Exemplar. … As really did He meet and resist the temptations of Satan as any of the children of humanity. … Jesus once stood in age just where you now stand, your circumstances, your cogitations at this period of your life, Jesus has had. … He is acquainted with your temptations" (*Our High Calling*, page 57). It is useless to say that Christ "met and resisted temptation" if He was not tempted.

Is any significant progress being made in the direction of unity?

We are all too close to the trees to see the forest very clearly. More important than any human judgment is the Biblical assurance that as we near the end of time God's people will come into unity. Truth unifies; error divides. Steadily, day by day, the knowledge of truth is bringing conviction to hearts everywhere throughout the church.

The encouraging word is that in the final disposition of the great controversy between Christ and Satan, truth will emerge fully triumphant. Thus there is every reason for confidence.

How is the "in Christ" idea of the New Testament related to the humanity of our Saviour?

Because "in Adam all die" (1 Corinthians 15:22), Christ had to take the nature of fallen Adam in order to qualify as the second or "last Adam." If He had taken the sinless nature of Adam before the fall, He could not have been our true Substitute, nor have died in order to redeem us.

In order to save the fallen sons and daughters of Adam, He must enter into the corporate stream of their fallen humanity, take their nature and mortality upon Himself, live therein the sinless life the law demands, submit to be "made … sin for us," and die the death that the broken law demands. There must be a reason why Jesus continually called Himself the Son of man! He must partake of the "flesh and blood," the nature, of "the children" of Adam (2 Corinthians 5:21; Hebrews 2:9-14).

As "all men" are legally in one man "in Adam," so all men are in One Man, in Christ. His life and His death are corporately ours to the benefit of the human race, our sin was "made to be" His so that we might be "made" the righteousness of God in Him. This union becomes effective in a change of heart and life when we believe.

Biblical justification by faith therefore is closely linked with the humanity of Christ. Failure to see this distorts the gospel itself.

QUESTIONS ABOUT THE HISTORY OF THE 1888 MESSAGE

Is the "1888 message" something passé like horse-drawn buggies and gas lamps?

One would normally think so. A tiny General Conference Session held a century ago would be unknown today (there were less than 100 delegates), except for one unforgettable happening. Ellen White tells the story:

> The Lord in His great mercy sent a most precious message to His people through Elders Waggoner and Jones. This message was to bring more prominently before the world the uplifted Saviour, the sacrifice for the sins of the whole world. It presented justification by faith in the Surety; it invited the people to receive the righteousness of Christ, which is made manifest in obedience to all the commandments of God (*Testimonies to Ministers and Gospel Workers*, pages 91, 92).

This message was "the beginning" of the long-promised latter rain and of the loud cry of Revelation 18 (*Special Testimonies*, Series A, No. 6, page 19; *Review and Herald*, November 22, 1892; Letter B2a, 1892). Those eschatological blessings have never yet been duplicated, because they bring in quick succession the final events.

Pentecost was the beginning of the "former rain" which has watered the souls of uncounted millions since the apostles' day. But the above statements declare the 1888 message to be the beginning of the final manifestation of what began at Pentecost. That's rather serious.

The story of how that message came, how it was received (or rejected), and what its content is, will fascinate Seventh-day Adventists until the gospel commission is completed. It has become an epic event of unparalleled significance, like the coming of the Messiah was to the

Jews 2000 years ago. The Jews have never been the same since, and neither has the Seventh-day Adventist Church been the same since 1888. The Holy Spirit will not let the history die.

I hear it said that the 1888 message is a nonentity, that it does not exist, because no one recorded Jones's and Waggoner's messages at the Minneapolis Conference. Could it be that all this talk about the 1888 message is in vain?

There is evidence that the message was indeed recorded. It is the on-going message that Ellen White endorsed wholeheartedly from 1888 through 1896, and even into 1897. She never limited her endorsements only to what was presented briefly at Minneapolis. Thus the actual message has not been "lost."

Ellen White's many on-going endorsements number in the hundreds if one counts all that are in the four-volume set of her 1,812 pages on the subject of 1888 (see Appendix). She never implied that Jones and Waggoner had lost their way between 1888 and 1896. Numerous *Signs* and *Review* articles also contained their on-going message. It is an insult to the character of God to say that He would grant such a blessing and allow it to be lost so we cannot recover it.

There are conflicting accounts of how the message was received a century ago. Some say it was accepted, some that it was rejected. Is it possible to know the facts?

Facts are stubborn entities that reasonable, candid human beings cannot deny. Facts regarding 1888 can be classified in three areas: the history of what happened; the content of the message itself; and the testimony of Ellen White.

Since Seventh-day Adventists believe that the Lord enabled her to exercise prophetic insight, her analysis of what happened has to be considered more accurate than the opinions of people who did not exercise that special gift. Contemporary conventional wisdom is not good enough.

Scores of times she declares emphatically that the message was rejected, not by the church at large but by the leadership of that day. Examples are: *Selected Messages*, book 1, pages 234, 235; *Testimonies to Ministers and Gospel Workers*, pages 63-81, 89-98.

As to the content of the message itself, objective analysis of our current teachings demonstrates that it has not yet been recovered. This will be seen as we consider further questions.

Why is this issue of 1888 so important? Can't we just go forward from here and forget the past?

The Jews cannot forget the history of Jesus Christ and go on as though nothing happened. They lost something when they rejected Him, and we lost something when we rejected the 1888 message. What we lost was "the third angel's message in verity" (*Review and Herald*, April 1, 1890). When Joseph and Mary through carelessness lost Jesus when returning from the Passover in Jerusalem, they had to go back and search for Him.

Not only must we recover what we lost; we must also learn our lesson so as not to repeat the same mistake again. George Santayana has said that "a nation that does not know its history is fated to repeat it" (*Saturday Evening Post*, September 27, 1958). Ken Burns, noted Civil War researcher, said: "The great arrogance of the present is to forget the intelligence of the past" (*American Heritage*, September-October, 1990). The German nation cannot blithely forget the Holocaust and go on as though nothing happened.

The God of heaven honored the Seventh-day Adventist Church by entrusting to our care the message of Revelation 18. That message was to lighten the earth with glory, to be the closing message of the gospel. It is painful for the Jews to think about Jesus of Nazareth; it is painful for the German nation to think about the Holocaust; it is also painful for us to think about 1888. But it is necessary.

If we choose to abandon the role that Heaven appointed us as a people, we can forget 1888 and go thoughtlessly on our way, seeking to maintain the status quo.

But if we wish to fulfill the role that Heaven has appointed us on the stage during earth's closing hours, we must recover what we lost.

What are the facts about how the 1888 message was accepted at the time, or rejected?

Sincere writers have maintained that it was accepted, and that it has been proclaimed clearly and powerfully ever since. If this is true, some disturbing questions demand answers:

• Why is the church generally still lukewarm 100 years after accepting that "beginning" of the latter rain and the loud cry?

• Why has not the gospel commission been completed and a people made ready for the second coming of Christ?

• Why hasn't the Lord returned?

If the message was "the beginning" of the loud cry of Revelation 18, then something must have gone wrong, for here we are over 100 years later when the loud cry was supposed to go "like fire in the stubble" (*Review and Herald*, December 15, 1885). Billions of people, including the Hindus and the Muslims, have hardly been touched with an intelligent grasp of "the third angel's message in verity." Neither has the message made a significant impact on Christendom.

Ellen White says that if the message had been accepted, the gospel commission could have been completed by 1893 (*General Conference Bulletin*, 1893, page 419). Some feel that she was naive to envisage such a possibility before the age of TV, jetliners, and computers. But they must forget that "the gospel ... is the power of God unto salvation." Many unbelieving Israelites doubted that David could slay Goliath with a pebble, but he did. And many doubted that Gideon's 300 could rout the Midianites, but they did.

A clear answer to this question of acceptance or rejection is possible:

(1) *History.* Historical research demonstrates that the majority of the delegates to the 1888 Session rejected the message. Their own acknowledgements are recorded in clear documentation.

In 1926, former president A. G. Daniells declared that up to that time the message had never been truly received or proclaimed. (Borrowing Evangelical concepts since that time has not filled the vacuum.) In 1988 Dr. Arnold Wallenkampf of the Biblical Research Institute published his *What Every Adventist Should Know About 1888*, in which he forcefully declares that leadership rejected the message and "insulted" the Holy Spirit. The February 1988 *Ministry* magazine published a similar article by Dr. Robert Olson of the White Estate.

The Centennial year of 1988 witnessed a further general about-face on this issue. No responsible scholar will now maintain the view of those authors of past decades who insisted that the message was accepted.

However, this is not to say that the message was rejected completely. There were a few at Minneapolis who believed it, and there have always been a few ever since who appreciate it. But Ellen White's testimony is consistent that "many" rejected and "few" accepted, and the "many" were those who directed the denomination's ministry. Hence our many years of wilderness wanderings, as Israel of old wandered so long before entering their Promised Land.

(2) *Theology.* The books, articles, and manuscripts produced after the 1888 Session by those delegates who rejected the message can be examined objectively. While they all professed to believe in "the doctrine of righteousness by faith," the theological content of their writings demonstrates that they did not proclaim the distinctive elements of that "most precious message" the Lord "sent."

For example, it is well-known that the principal opponent, Uriah Smith, maintained his opposition until his death in 1903. Yet he insisted that he had always believed in justification by faith. Many agreed with him in his opposition views. His writings from 1888 through 1903 demonstrate that he never accepted the message. When a controversy erupted in 1906-1907 over the two covenants, most of our General Conference and publishing house leaders opted to defend the view held by the opponents of the message in 1890. Such incidents demonstrate an on-going rejection.

Ellen White said that even if opposing brethren should repent of rejecting the message (which few completely did), they could never recover what they lost (Letter, January 9, 1893). This loss is evident in reading their writings. When the new century dawned in 1900, virtually no one was proclaiming the message except the original three, Jones, Waggoner, and Ellen White.

(3) *Ellen White's testimony.* In scores of statements, perhaps even hundreds, Ellen White states that the 1888 message which "the Lord in His great mercy sent" was "in a great degree" rejected by our brethren, and that the rejection continued on through 1901. Here are a few out of many examples:

> Again and again did I bear my testimony to those assembled [Minneapolis, 1888] in a clear and forcible manner, but that testimony was not received. When I came to Battle Creek … not one … had the courage to stand on my side and help Elder Butler to see that he, as well as others, had taken wrong positions. … The prejudice of Elder Butler was greater after hearing the various reports from our ministering brethren at that meeting in Minneapolis (Letter U3, 1889).

For nearly two years we have been urging the people to come up and accept the light and the truth concerning the righteousness of Christ, and they do not know whether to come and take hold of this precious truth or not. … Our young men look to our older brethren, and as they see that they do not accept the message, but treat it as though it were of no consequence, it influences those who are ignorant of the Scriptures to reject the light. These men who refuse to receive truth, interpose themselves between the people and the light (*Review and Herald*, March 11, 18, 1892).

We should be the last people on earth to indulge in the slightest degree the spirit of persecution against those who are bearing the message of God to the world. This is the most terrible feature of unchristlikeness that has manifested itself among us since the Minneapolis meeting (Letter 25b, 1892).

Who of those that acted a part in the meeting at Minneapolis have come to the light and received the rich treasures of truth which the Lord sent them from heaven? … Who have made full confession of their mistaken zeal, their blindness, their jealousies and evil surmisings, their defiance of truth? Not one … (Letter B2a, 1892).

At Minneapolis … the light that is to lighten the whole earth with its glory was resisted, and by the action of our own brethren has been in a great degree kept away from the world (*Selected Messages*, book 1, pages 234, 235; 1896).

Although there were brief revivals as the result of the combined ministry of Ellen White, Jones, and Waggoner during 1889 and 1890, the Battle Creek-inspired opposition finally won the day. The 1896 statement above is conclusive.

But this does not mean that the church is in a hopeless state of apostasy. Repentance is possible; and the Lord Jesus Christ calls for it (Revelation 3:19). Modern Israel must rehearse the significance of her history and learn its lessons, as the ancient Israelites after decades of wandering rehearsed theirs before they could enter their Promised Land. We have come to the time when an antitypical "Deuteronomy" must take place.

It is difficult to understand how Seventh-day Adventist church leaders a century ago could have done anything comparable to what the Jews did to Christ. This seems unbelievable!

The following are only a few of many similar statements by Ellen White:

> Those who resisted the Spirit of God at Minneapolis [1888] were waiting for a chance to travel over the same ground again, because the spirit was the same. … All the universe of heaven witnessed the disgraceful treatment of Jesus Christ, represented by the Holy Spirit. Had Christ been before them, they would have treated Him in a manner similar to that in which the Jews treated Christ (Series A, No. 6, page 20; January 16, 1896).[1]

> If you reject Christ's delegated [1888] messengers, you reject Christ (*Testimonies to Ministers and Gospel Workers*, page 97).

Isn't there a danger that disclosing the truth of this history may weaken the people's confidence in the leadership of the church?

Through one means or another, it is inevitable that eventually the people (and the world itself) must learn the full truth. Abraham Lincoln said, "You can fool some of the people all the time; you can fool all of the people some of the time; but you cannot fool all of the people all the time." Full disclosure must come sometime. It has been impossible not to let the world know the full story of the Jews' failure.

If leadership recognize the truth of our history, the people's confidence in them cannot be impaired, for everyone knows that human beings are not perfect or infallible. Repentance is still possible, and the

---

1. Other such statements are found in MSS 9, 15, 1888; *Through Crisis to Victory*, pages 292, 297, 300; MS 13, 1889; *Review and Herald*, March 4, 11, August 26, 1890, April 11, 18, 1893; *Testimonies to Ministers and Gospel Workers*, pages 64, 65, 75-80. See also The *Ellen G. White 1888 Materials*, pages 529, 530. Once she likened the rejection of the 1888 message to the rebellion of Korah, Dathan, and Abram (page 600).

church at large will support a program of honest repentance. Confidence can be impaired only if leadership should try to deny the obvious facts of history, deny responsibility, and refuse Christ's call to repentance.

The Bible tells the full truth of the history of God's people, never glossing over the failures of leaders. To recognize our mistakes of a century ago is not to discredit today's leaders in the least. It illuminates the darkened corners of our understanding as to why time has gone on so long when the coming of the Lord was due a century ago. "Ye shall know the truth, and the truth shall make you free," said Jesus to Jews of His day. His words apply also to our dilemma now of trying to explain why the Lord has not intervened to end the on-going agonies of this planet. His honor and vindication are at stake.

It seems almost impossible to believe that church leaders could reject the beginning of the outpouring of the latter rain, for which they had been praying for decades. How could they do this?

For the same reason that the Jews rejected their Messiah when they had been expecting Him for over a thousand years. Ellen White declares that it was the same sin of unbelief.

Such unbelief is the phenomenon of the ages. It prevented the Jewish leaders from recognizing Him as a baby in the humble manger in the stable in Bethlehem, although the shepherds and wise men did recognize Him. Throughout His ministry in lowly circumstances, the proud Jews would not "believe," because faith always requires a humbling of the human heart.

Ellen White declares that our real problem in 1888 and thereafter was that mysterious sin of unbelief, the proud love of self:

> If the rays of light which shone at Minneapolis were permitted to exert their convincing power upon those who took their stand against light, … they would have had a rich experience; but self said "No." Self was not willing to be bruised; self struggled for the mastery. … Self and passion developed hateful characteristics (Letter 019, 1892).

She added later that "that wonderful 'I'" was what attempted "to put down the Holy Spirit's teaching" (*Testimonies to Ministers and Gospel Workers*, p. 70). We today partake of the same human nature as did they. We are no better than they were. We must wrestle with that same problem, and we shall certainly fail again and again unless and until we learn this lesson.

We are told that the real work of justification by faith is to lay the glory of man in the dust, and to do for him that which he cannot do for himself (*Review and Herald*, September 16, 1902). This is what faith does for the human heart:

> When I survey the wondrous cross
> On which the Prince of glory died
> My richest gain I count but loss,
> And pour contempt on all my pride.
> —*Isaac Watts*

Unbelief does the opposite. It nurtures personal, professional, and denominational pride. That was the problem in 1888.

Is the same mistake being made today that was made a century ago?

Because our human nature is the same as that of our predecessors, it is impossible for us to not make the same mistake again unless we have learned our lesson from the past. It is impossible for the Jews of today not to repeat the mistake of their forefathers who rejected Christ unless they learn the lesson of their history. Human nature is the same in all generations, and it will surely act out again its characteristics unless full repentance is received.

For decades the world Seventh-day Adventist Church has not known the full truth of our 1888 history, because that truth was repeatedly skewed and misreported. The popular misconception has been two-fold:

(1) The false assumption that the 1888 message was received and is therefore our secure possession today. This has been a very popular error because it serves to minimize the sin of the rejectors and thus minimizes our own sin in repeating it.

(2) The false assumption that the message was only a "re-emphasis" of the teachings of the 16th-century Reformers and of contemporary Evangelicals. This has nurtured a feeling of being "rich and increased with goods, ... [in] need of nothing." Pride is highly popular.

These two widely prevalent errors would make it inevitable that a process of rejection should take place again today *if* in God's providence the message should be recovered and again presented in its freshness, and if repentance should be rejected.

However, Christ died for the redemption of His church. His grace operating on human hearts purifies them from the love of self, and imparts a basic honesty that will recognize and confess truth once it is made apparent.

Since the truth of our 1888 history has begun to be officially published in 1988, a change is sure to take place. The complete release by the White Estate of all that Ellen White said about this history is a step in the right direction (1,812 pages in four volumes). The Holy Spirit has always blessed her testimony. All that God's honest people need in order to open their hearts to receive God's gift of repentance is the full knowledge of that truth. There are hopeful signs that it cannot be forever suppressed.

Opposition will of course manifest itself in unexpected quarters; a "shaking" is necessary. But in the final battle between truth and error, God must have a people for whom truth will prevail. Otherwise, the plan of salvation is lost and the world itself is doomed.

Jesus said, "By their fruits ye shall know them." What kind of fruit did the 1888 message bear in the years immediately after the Minneapolis Conference?

Ellen White speaks thus of the "fruit" the message bore in those early days, in the face of official opposition:

> I saw that the power of God attended the message wherever it was spoken. You could not make the people believe in South Lancaster that it was not a message of light that came to them. The people confessed their sins, and appropriated the righteousness of Christ. God has set His hand to do this work. … The blessing of God swept over us [Jones, Waggoner, and herself in Chicago] as we pointed men [and women] to the Lamb of God that taketh away the sin of the world. … How long will those at the head of the work keep themselves aloof from the message of God? (*Review and Herald*, March 18,1890).

Now although there has been a determined effort to make of no effect the message God has sent, its fruits have been proving that it was from the source of light and truth. Those who have cherished unbelief and prejudice, who in place of helping to do the work the Lord would have them do, have stood to bar the way against all evidence, cannot be supposed to have clearer spiritual eyesight for having so long closed their eyes to the light God sent to the people (Letter O-19, 1892).

The universal testimony from those who have spoken has been that this message of light and truth which has come to our people is just the truth for this time and wherever they [Jones and Waggoner] go among the churches, light, and relief, and the blessing of God is sure to come in (MS 10, 1889).

After the Minneapolis meeting how wonderfully the Spirit of God wrought; men confessed that they had robbed God by withholding tithes and offerings. Many souls were converted. Thousands of dollars were brought into the treasury. Rich experiences were related by those whose hearts were aglow with the love of God (MS 22, 1890).

Note the dates of these statements: 1889, 1890. These wonderful revivals ceased when the opposition snuffed out the work of the Holy Spirit. The General Conference soon scattered the team. In 1891, Ellen White herself was exiled to Australia, and the following year Waggoner was virtually exiled to England. But the brief but abortive revivals described above have forever testified that the message was indeed from the Lord.

I have read reports that Jones and/or Waggoner were harsh, rude, and unchristlike, themselves to blame for the opposition they had to endure. If so, the brethren who rejected their message did not commit so serious a sin; and furthermore ... we today, can we not be excused if we reject the message again?

Several facts constitute an answer to this question:

(1) As an inspired prophet, Ellen White speaks of "the sin" that the rejecting brethren "committed in what took place in Minneapolis" (Letter O-19, 1892). She could hardly have said that if she thought that the two messengers were in any way to blame for the rejection.

(2) She speaks of Waggoner in 1888 as "a Christian gentleman" (MS 15, 1888).

(3) She speaks of Jones presenting his message with "light, with grace, and power" (Letter, January 9, 1893). In his messages and in the way he delivered them, "the people … saw the truth, goodness, mercy, and love of God as they never before had seen it" *(Review and Herald,* February 12, 1889). She said further that he set "forth the message with beauty and loveliness, to charm all whose hearts are not closed with prejudice" (ibid., May 27, 1890). When it became necessary in a certain crisis for him to mention the opposition of his brethren, "Brother Jones talked very plainly, yet tenderly" (Letter W84, 1890).

His voluminous sermons at the 1893 and 1895 General Conference sessions are recorded stenographically in the *Bulletins* and are readily available today for anyone to read. According to Ellen White, only a "prejudiced" mind can find evidence therein of harshness or rudeness.

(4) Jones and Waggoner had something no other Adventist minister in history is known to have had—"heavenly credentials" *(Review and Herald,* March 18, 1890; MS 9, 1890).

But is there no record of Jones being abrupt and harsh?

Nearly forty years after the event, one critic reported that on one occasion during the Minneapolis meetings Jones spoke disrespectfully to Uriah Smith. No one knows for sure even if the alleged remark was partly in jest. Ellen White never mentioned the incident in her diary, indicating that she thought it a minor episode. There is abundant evidence that Jones's general attitude in those years was that of a sincere, humble, kind-hearted Christian.

For sure, both "messengers" were fallible men, "only men," Ellen White says (as are all of us). We must beware lest we bear false witness against them in an effort to discredit their message and ministry.

It is a well-known fact that both Jones and Waggoner lost their way eventually. Does this indicate there is something wrong with their message?

It is true that they did begin to lose their way about the turn of the century. And then Jones began to let drops of gall get into his spirit, which brought forth rebukes from Ellen White. Eventually he lost confidence in General Conference leadership, and his spirit became wrong. Waggoner lost faith in the sanctuary message, and suffered a domestic tragedy.

What must be borne in mind is that Ellen White's endorsements of their message and ministry continued from 1888 through 1896. She insisted that their later failures cannot fairly be blamed on their earlier message.

Ellen White specifically said that if they should eventually lose their way, their opposers (with feelings of "enmity," she says), would seize upon this tragedy as an excuse to reject their message and thus would "triumph." But in so doing, they would "enter upon a fatal delusion" (Letters O-19; S24, 1892). The last thing we want today is such a "delusion."

We must recognize however that neither Jones or Waggoner ever gave up their faith in Christ or their love for the Sabbath truth. In today's climate of church fellowship standards they would probably remain in membership.

Why did Jones and Waggoner lose their spiritual power?

The reason Ellen White gives is that their opposers treated them so unfairly and even "cruelly" that they almost forced them to stumble:

> The suspicion and jealousy, the evil surmising, the resistance of the Spirit of God that was appealing to them, were more after the order in which the reformers had been treated. It was the very order in which the [Methodist] church had treated my father's family and eight of us. ... I stated that the course that had been pursued at Minneapolis was cruelty to the Spirit of God (MS 30, 1889).

> It is not the inspiration from heaven that leads one to be suspicious, watching for a chance and greedily seizing upon it to prove that those brethren who differ from us in some interpretations of Scripture are not sound in the faith. There is danger that this course of action will produce the very result assumed; and to a great degree the guilt will rest upon those who are watching for evil. ...

The opposition in our own ranks has imposed upon the Lord's messengers [Jones and Waggoner] a laborious and soul trying task (*General Conference Bulletin*, 1893, pages 419- 421).

Granted that they were mistreated; was that an excuse for their failure?

No. Sin is never excusable in anyone. But what they had to endure was what she called "unchristlike persecution" (ibid., page 184).

Of course, even enduring persecution is never an excuse for sin. But their trial was incomparably more severe spiritually than was that of Martin Luther who suffered persecution from the pope, the cardinals and bishops. Luther could rejoice in his persecutions because he recognized the papacy as the "little horn" of Daniel 7 and the "beast" of Revelation 13. But Jones and Waggoner could find no such comfort. They knew that this is the true "remnant" church of prophecy. No eighth church is to follow Laodicea. And overcoming, not spiritual failure, is what the prophecy says must come.

The terrible rejection of "the beginning" of the latter rain and the loud cry was something they could not understand. It was totally outside God's plan for the closing up of the great controversy issues. Heaven was astonished, for even the angels did not expect this phenomenal reaction against the Holy Spirit, even to the point of "cruelty" and "insulting" Him at a General Conference Session.

Such bitter opposition to Him should have ended at the close of the 1260 years of persecution. According to Ellen White, this was the first time that the leadership of the Seventh-day Adventist Church firmly set themselves against the much more abounding grace of Christ, repeated the sin of the ancient Jews, and in the process even rejected her own ministry.

But weren't Jones and Waggoner strong men who should have endured their trial?

It is not surprising that there were casualties, for Jones and Waggoner were weak men as are we all. That must have been one reason why the Lord called them to their special work, for He cannot easily use "strong" people. He told Paul that "my strength is made perfect in weakness" (2 Corinthians 12:9). They were not prophets as was Ellen White, and each was only a man. A woman was able to endure the trial, although she too suffered greatly.

And their understanding was not only finite, it was restricted by an apparent lack of Scriptural or prophetic information to explain what was happening. It was a Great Disappointment more mysterious even than that of 1844. They could not understand, nor could they possibly foresee another century of violent human history and agony having to go by. Thus they lost their "bearings," says Ellen White.

Before we castigate them, we would do well to ask ourselves if we could have endured that bitter experience any better. The most painful trial that any loyal Seventh-day Adventist can endure must be that of determined and persistent opposition from church leadership. Nevertheless, the grace of the Lord was and is always sufficient.

That trial was essentially the same that Joseph had to endure when his ten brethren opposed him, and what David had to endure from King Saul, and what Jeremiah had to endure from Kings Jehoikim and Zedekiah and the priests and "prophets" of his day. Jones and Waggoner had to suffer; and to their shame they failed to endure successfully.

Another reason can well be that the light they had was only "the beginning" of the final outpouring of the Holy Spirit. That beginning was not enough to enable them to endure a spiritual test that no previous servants of God had been called to endure. Such "unchristlike persecution" initiated by church leadership during the antitypical Day of Atonement is unprecedented in sacred history. Heaven and hell must both have marveled at the success that Satan gained (see *Selected Messages*, book 1, pages 234, 235).

It is a solemn thought that "the Lord, whose name is Jealous, is a jealous God" (Exodus 34:14). In these last days of the great controversy, He will give anyone who wants them hooks on which to hang their doubts (*The Great Controversy*, page 527). That is a severe generosity! It seems that that mysterious divine "jealousy" will let us invent every possible stumbling block as an excuse to reject His true latter rain and accept a counterfeit.

There is wonderful progress of the church worldwide in baptizing large numbers of people and erecting fine institutions. Is this sufficient evidence that repentance is unnecessary?

For many decades we as a church have rejoiced at such progress. This has repeatedly been cited as evidence that we do not need to recover the 1888 message—or as evidence that we already possess it.

However, there are other denominations making even more spectacular "progress." The Roman church is increasing its membership far more than we are, and erecting finer buildings, as are certain Protestant, especially Pentecostal, groups. Even the Mormons and Jehovah's Witnesses make progress. And Islam is growing by leaps and bounds.

The strength of the church is not in its statistical or financial records. We were never called to accumulate statistics and institutions to impress the world, but to proclaim a message that would prepare a people for the coming of the Lord. If we were to baptize every human soul in the entire world and make each one to be a lukewarm church member as most of us are today, that would not hasten the coming of the Lord.

The test of our true progress is spiritual growth. A Good News message that is truly powerful must lighten the earth. There must be a preparation to meet the final issues—the mark of the beast and the close of probation. Heaven is better prepared to evaluate our progress accurately than are we.

One hint that we do have is Christ's message to Laodicea—the startling disclosure (in the Greek) that of all the seven churches of history, we are the one who is *outstandingly* "wretched, and miserable, and poor, and blind, and naked," while we think ourselves "rich, and increased with goods."

Since Jones and Waggoner did eventually lose their way, is it not dangerous for us to read their writings?

Their writings are never at any time to be considered as inspired or as a part of the canon. The Bible alone is to have that honor.

But Ellen White said that they discovered "precious ore" in "the mines of truth." We are not to preach Jones and Waggoner, neither are we called to preach Ellen White. We are to preach the Bible, but to accept all the light that the Lord has seen fit to send us.

"The Lord in His great mercy sent" Jones and Waggoner with "a most precious message." The Holy Spirit gave them insight into Bible truths that our people had not previously discerned. In over a hundred years of scrutiny and frequent opposition, no competent scholar has pinpointed any important aspect of their message from 1888 through 1896 that is not clearly supported by Scripture.

At what point do their writings become unreliable?

Waggoner's studies on Hebrews at the 1897 General Conference Session contain many helpful insights, but he began to express some confusing thoughts suggesting panentheism. Likewise, the original edition of *The Glad Tidings* (1900) had some such thoughts, although in 1901 he denied believing or teaching pantheism. When the Pacific Press republished it in 1972, these confusing statements were taken out, leaving his basic message of righteousness by faith intact and in harmony with his previous writings.

According to the records, Jones uttered no pantheistic or panentheistic thoughts. But after about 1904 he began to lose confidence in General Conference leadership. However, his *The Consecrated Way to Christian Perfection* was for the most part written before 1900 (parts of it as early as 1894), and contains none of the drops of gall that got into his writings after 1905.

In their later writings both doubt the possibility of denominational repentance, and this is the deciding factor that led to their failure. (And any movement or "independent ministry" that doubts that possibility must likewise fail.)

Neither Jones nor Waggoner ever repudiated the 1888 message; neither gave up the Sabbath, or lost his love for Christ and the Bible. As Ellen White said, error in their later writings cannot cancel the truth in their earlier writings. Good common sense is always appropriate. We do not refuse to read the Psalms because of David's failures and mistakes.

What is the difference between Christ dwelling in the believing heart through faith, and His dwelling in every person's heart?

There is a fine line between the truth of John 1:9 which says that Christ is "the Light which lighteth every man that cometh into the world," and the panentheism doctrine that Christ personally dwells in "every man" before he exercises faith and is converted. That idea was not a part of the 1888-1896 message that Ellen White endorsed.

Some charge that the 1888 message leads into pantheism. But there was no pantheism in the message which Ellen White endorsed, and there is nothing in it that leads to pantheism.

Paul often speaks of Christ dwelling in the heart, but he is speaking of believers, not unbelievers (cf. 2 Corinthians 13:5). Paul does not say that God's Son was in him even before his conversion," but that God chose him from the womb (Galatians 1:15, 16).

The revealing of His Son in Paul was following his conversion. And that revealing was not an unfolding of what was there in his heart all along, unrealized. The mistaken New Age idea is borrowed from Hinduism, that God is within you waiting only to be realized. Christ entered Paul's heart to abide there *at his conversion.* But the Light was indeed shining on his heart all his life, while resisted.

One text often misunderstood is thought to support the New Age idea: "The kingdom of God is within you" (Luke 17:20, 21). Jesus informed the Jews that although they had been looking for the kingdom of God to come, here it was manifested among them, or "in the midst of you," undiscerned. He did not say that God dwelt within them as unbelievers.

There is a "power working from within, a new life from above, … Christ … [quickening] the lifeless faculties of the soul" (*Steps to Christ,* page 18). But this work of the Holy Spirit within the heart leads toward conversion and sanctification.

5

QUESTIONS ABOUT THE TWO COVENANTS

These have always been confusing to me. What is the difference between the old covenant and the new covenant?

This was a key element of the 1888 message and a controversial one. Simply put, here is the essence of the view of Jones and Waggoner which was so different from the view of the brethren.

The new covenant is the same as "the everlasting covenant," and is the promise of God to save us, not our promise to obey Him. The Lord made this promise to Abraham and to his descendants in Genesis 12:1-3; 13:14-17; 15:5; 22:16-18.

The promise included (1) the earth for an everlasting possession, (2) everlasting life so they could enjoy it, and (3) righteousness by faith with all its attendant blessings. In short, God virtually promised Abraham the sky. All the latter did in response was to "believe." The Lord required nothing more of him, and He counted his faith for righteousness (Genesis 15:6). *That is the simple story of the new covenant.*

The old covenant is backwards from that. Four hundred and thirty years later Abraham's descendants were gathered at Mount Sinai on their way to the Promised Land. Through Moses, the Lord renewed the promise to them. However, they did not have the faith of Abraham. Instead of responding as he did, they manifested pride and self-sufficiency, making the vain promise, "All that the Lord hath spoken we will do" (Exodus 19:8). *That promise of the people is the simple story of the old covenant.*

The Lord could not abandon His people at Mount Sinai. If they would not keep step with Him, He must keep step with them. Therefore in the next chapter of Exodus He came down on Mount Sinai with thunder, lightning, an earthquake and fire, and spoke the

Ten Commandments and wrote them on tables of stone. Then He instituted the entire Levitical system.

Because Abraham "believed," the Lord did not have to do that to him; instead, He wrote the law in his heart.

Nevertheless, the Lord maintained a gracious purpose in it for the unbelieving Israelites. "... the law was our schoolmaster [truant officer, disciplinarian] to bring us unto Christ, that we might be justified by faith," as was Abraham (Galatians 3:24). According to Paul's brilliant insight, the long detour of centuries was needed in order to bring the people to the faith which Abraham exercised in the beginning.

In brief, how does the 1888 idea of the two covenants differ from the common idea held today?

The common idea is that the old and new covenants represent two dispensations in God's plan. The old covenant was to be valid up to the time of Christ, and then the new covenant would come into force.

But the 1888 messengers saw a deeper truth: the two covenants are not matters of time, but of condition. There were people in Old Testament times who lived under the new covenant, for they had faith in Christ as did Abraham; there are Christians today living under the old covenant, because they do not exercise the faith of Abraham.

Where can we find a clear presentation of the 1888 view of the two covenants?

In chapters 3 and 4 of *The Glad Tidings* by E. J. Waggoner. Ellen White's view in *Patriarchs and Prophets*, chapter 32, supports Waggoner's view. There is also a chapter presenting the same view in *Grace on Trial: The Heartwarming Message the Lord "Sent" to Us*, by Robert J. Wieland, chapter 9; Glad Tidings Publishers, 2001.

Did Ellen White comment about E. J. Waggoner's The Glad Tidings?

We do not know that Ellen White ever said anything about *The Glad Tidings* as a book (a verse-by-verse commentary on Galatians); but she made many enthusiastic comments about Waggoner's studies in Galatians 12 years earlier. His righteousness-by-faith views of Galatians and the two covenants did not change during those 12 years.

Dr. L. E. Froom tells us that Waggoner's widow took down his Minneapolis talks in shorthand, transcribed them, and that he published them in 1889 *Signs of the Times* articles, *Christ and His Righteousness* (1890), and *The Glad Tidings* (1900; see *Movement of Destiny*, pages 189–201).

What specific comments does Ellen White make about the 1888 view of the two covenants?

Ellen White firmly supported Waggoner's view of the two covenants:

> I am much pleased to learn that Professor Prescott is giving the same lessons in his class to the students that Brother [E. J.] Waggoner has been giving. He is presenting the covenants. John thinks it is presented in a clear and convincing manner.
>
> Since I made the statement last Sabbath that the view of the covenants as it had been taught by Brother Waggoner was truth, it seems that great relief has come to many minds.
>
> I am inclined to think Brother Prescott receives the testimony, although he was not present when I made this statement. I thought it time to take my position, and I am glad that the Lord urged me to give the testimony that I did (Letter 30, 1890).
>
> Night before last, the Lord opened many things to my mind. It was plainly revealed what your influence has been, what it was in Minneapolis. ...
>
> You have strengthened the hands and minds of such men as Larson, Porter, Dan Jones, Eldridge and Morrison and Nicola and a vast number of them. All quote you, and the enemy of righteousness looks on pleased. ...
>
> You are by your influence doing what other men have done before you, closing the door to your own soul where if God should send light from heaven, not one ray would penetrate to your soul because you closed the door so it should not find access there. ...
>
> Do not labor so hard to do the very work Satan is doing. This work was done in Minneapolis. Satan triumphed. This work has been done here [Battle Creek].
>
> Night before last I was shown that evidences in regard to the covenants were clear and convincing. Yourself, Dan Jones, Brother Porter and others are spending your investigative powers for naught to produce a position on the covenants to vary from the position that Brother Waggoner has presented.

When you had received the true light which shineth, you would have not imitated or gone over the same manner of interpretation and misconstruing the Scriptures that [sic] did the Jews. ... They handled those things that they could make a means of clouding and misleading minds.

The covenant question is a clear question and would be received by every candid, unprejudiced mind, but I was brought where the Lord gave me an insight into this matter. You have turned from plain light because you were afraid that the law question in Galatians would have to be accepted (Letter to Uriah Smith, 59, 1890).

Why do our Seventh-day Adventist Bible Commentary and Bible Dictionary follow the view of those who opposed the 1888 message a century ago?

Some of the editors may have been sincerely uninformed about the 1888 view which Ellen White endorsed. There is also evidence that some decidedly opposed the 1888 view.

Does the following comment from Ellen White disagree with E. J. Waggoner's view of the two covenants in The Glad Tidings (pages 71-87)?

This is the pledge that God's people are to make in these last days. Their acceptance with God depends on a faithful fulfillment of the terms of their agreement with Him. God includes in His covenant all who will obey Him (*Seventh-day Adventist Bible Commentary*, vol. 1, page 1103; *Review and Herald*, June 23, 1904).

Some believe that this does disagree with Waggoner's presentation. It appears that she is teaching and supporting the old covenant of "obey and live," which Paul says "gendereth to bondage" (Galatians 4:24). She appears to be endorsing the view of the brethren who rejected Waggoner's view of the new covenant message, such as Uriah Smith, Dan T. Jones, G. I. Butler, R. C. Porter, R. M. Kilgore, and others (cf. Robert J. Wieland, *1888 Re-examined*, pages 45-49). It *appears* so. However, her view in *Patriarchs and Prophets* clearly supports Waggoner.

Some of her statements on the nature of Christ also *appear superficially* to be contradictory and to support the popular view that

Christ took only the sinless nature of Adam before the fall. But when studied carefully in context, these apparently conflicting statements are seen to be not self-contradictory.

There are others of her statements on the two covenants that are as clear as sunlight and cannot be misinterpreted or misunderstood. This one becomes clear from a careful reading in context. Will Ellen White contradict what she wrote 14 years earlier? She can hardly build credibility if she does.

Her clearest writing on the two covenants is in *Patriarchs and Prophets*, pages 370-373, where her position is in full harmony with Waggoner's. Thus, with three clearly unequivocal statements in support of Waggoner's view, how shall we understand the 1904 statement which *appears* to contradict it?

(1) Note the context of the 1904 statement. When the Lord says "My covenant" in Isaiah 56:4, He is clearly referring to the covenant He made with Abraham—the "new covenant." When God makes a covenant, it is always a promise; and it is always one-sided. He never asks us to make promises in return, for He knows we cannot keep our promises. We cannot deal with God on equal terms. Ellen White goes on to say, "This is the covenant spoken of in the following scripture" (Exodus 19:1-8). She is referring to the Lord's covenant, not the people's promise. Says Ellen White in 1904:

"Ye have seen what I did unto the Egyptians, and how I bare you on eagles' wings, and brought you unto Myself. Now therefore, if ye will obey My voice indeed"—in truth, earnestness, and sincerity,—"and keep My covenant. ..."

(2) The only covenant which the Lord mentions here refers to His covenant, His promise, to Abraham. Thus it is clear that the Lord was proposing to renew the *new* covenant or righteousness by faith with the people at Mount Sinai, not to institute an *old* one of legalism.

(3) The Hebrew word here for "obey" means to "listen," to "hear, hearken" (*shamea*, cf. any lexicon or Young). The word for "keep" is a cognate word (*shamar*). It is not the usual word for "obey" or "do." It has the root meaning of "take heed" or "cherish." For example, Adam was to "dress and to keep" (*shamar*) the Garden of Eden (Genesis 2:15). He could not be said to "*obey* or *do* the Garden," but to *cherish* it. The word *shamar* connotes the beautiful idea of *appreciation*.

(4) Thus what the Lord said to Israel was, "Now therefore, if you will listen to My voice indeed in truth, earnestness and sincerity, and cherish or *appreciate* the covenant I made with your father Abraham ... ," all these good things will happen and you will be a "kingdom of priests," etc. All of Abraham's true descendants were to have the heartfelt faith of Abraham. The Lord never intended them to institute a program of salvation by works. Nor would Ellen White dare to change a righteousness-by-faith text into a legalism one.

(5) Her use of the word "pledge" must therefore mean "commitment." In other words, God desired from the people the same response that Abraham made, a choice to believe the Lord and to cooperate with Him. Yet he made no vain promise as did Israel 430 years later. He gave *his heart* to the Lord, exercising faith in the Saviour to come. Such a choice to believe and yield the heart is what Ellen White means by "pledge."

(6) Ellen White's context in her 1904 article is clear: "Christ calls upon the members of his church to cherish the true, genuine hope of *the gospel.*" Note her unconscious use of the Hebrew idea of *shamea*— the word "cherish," which we find in Exodus 19.

It is unthinkable that the inspired prophet should contradict what she said in *Steps to Christ*, page 47. Here she tells of the tragic result of living under the old covenant, making promises to God that He never requires, and which drag us into bondage:

Your promises and resolutions are like ropes of sand. You cannot control your thoughts, your impulses, your affections. The knowledge of your broken promises and forfeited pledges weakens your confidence in your own sincerity, and causes you to feel that God cannot accept you; but you need not despair.

Is it true that agape is a prominent element of the 1888 message? Or is this something that modern enthusiasts have added to it?

Waggoner speaks thus about *agape*:

"Now the end of the commandment is charity out of a pure heart, and of a good conscience, and of faith unfeigned." The word here rendered "charity" is often rendered "love," and is so rendered in this place in the New Version [R.V].

In 1 John 5:3 we read: "This is the love of God, that we keep His commandments;" and Paul himself says that "love is the fulfilling of the law." Romans 13:10. In both these texts the same word (*agape*) is used that occurs in 1 Timothy 1:5. ...

God imputes to believers the righteousness of Christ, who was made in the likeness of sinful flesh, so that "the righteousness of the law" might be fulfilled in their lives. And thus Christ is the end of the law (*The Bible Echo*, February 15, 1892; *Lessons on Faith*, pages 69-71).

What glory there is in the cross! All the glory of heaven is in that despised thing. Not in the figure of the cross, but in the cross itself. ...

"Where'er I go, I'll tell the story
Of the cross, of the cross;
In nothing else my soul shall glory,
Save the cross, save the cross;
And this my constant theme shall be,
Through time and in eternity,
That Jesus tasted death for me
On the cross, on the cross."
— *The Glad Tidings*, pages 143, 144

Writing under the special blessing of the 1888 message, Ellen White said:

Since the General Conference of 1888, Satan has been working with special power through unconsecrated elements to weaken the confidence of God's people in the voice that has been appealing to them for these many years. ...

There is one great central truth to be kept ever before the mind ... Christ and Him crucified. ... The soul palsied by sin can be endowed with life only through the work wrought out upon the cross by the Author of our salvation. The love of Christ constrains man to unite with Him in His labors and sacrifice. The revelation of divine love awakens in them a sense of their neglected obligation to be light-bearers to the world, and inspires them with a missionary spirit. This truth enlightens the mind and sanctifies the soul. It will banish unbelief and inspire faith. It is the one great truth to be constantly kept before the minds of men. Yet how dimly is the love of God understood; and in the teaching of the word it makes but a faint impression (MS 31, 1890; *The Ellen G. White 1888 Materials*, pages 805, 806).

NOTES

6

QUESTIONS ABOUT UNKNOWN SIN

Is there such a thing as unconscious sin? Does the 1888 message speak of it?

We know that the most terrible sin ever committed was an unknown sin. Jesus prayed for those who crucified Him, "Father, forgive them; for they know not what they do" (Luke 23:34).

To "know not" something is to be unconscious of it. And to blame the Jews and the Romans for that crime is shortsighted, for we all partake of that guilt (*Testimonies to Ministers and Gospel Workers*, page 38; *The Desire of Ages*, page 745). Yet the human race is still not conscious of that sin.

Laodicea's pride is likewise an unknown sin, for the True Witness says, "Thou ... knowest not" (Revelation 3:17). King Hezekiah did not know of the evil buried in his heart when he was sick unto death. That evil came to the surface after he was healed. "God left him, to try him, that he might know all that was in his heart" (2 Chronicles 32:31).

David prayed a better prayer than did Hezekiah, "Search me, O God, and know my heart: try me, and know my thoughts; and see if there be any wicked way in me ..." (Psalm 139:23, 24).

Yes, the 1888 messengers did speak of unknown sin being brought to consciousness by the Holy Spirit's ministry on this Day of Atonement.

Where in the 1888 message itself do we find this idea expressed?

When sin is pointed out to you, say, "I would rather have Christ than that." And let it go. [Congregation: "Amen."] ... Then where ... is the opportunity for any of us to get discouraged over our sins? Now some of the brethren here have done that very thing. They came here free; but the Spirit of God brought up something they never saw before. The Spirit of God went deeper than it ever went before, and revealed things they never saw before; and then, instead of thanking the Lord that that was so, and letting the whole wicked business go, ... they began to get discouraged. ...

If the Lord has brought up sins to us that we never thought of before, that only shows that He is going down to the depths, and He will reach the bottom at last; and when He finds the last thing that is unclean or impure, that is out of harmony with His will, and brings that up, and shows that to us, and we say, "I would rather have the Lord than that"—then the work is complete, and the seal of the living God can be fixed upon that character. ... Let Him go on, brethren; let Him keep on His searching work (A. T. Jones, *General Conference Bulletin*, 1893, page 404).

But we have always thought that if we confess our sins, our hearts are then totally cleansed, and there can be no remaining unknown sin.

"If we confess our sins, He is faithful and just to forgive us our sins, and to cleanse us from all unrighteousness" (1 John 1:9). Very true; but let us please note that He cannot forgive and cleanse sins that we do not *understandably* confess. Sin is not magically cleansed like we press an erase button on a computer.

Confession must be specific and conscious: the sinner "shall confess that he hath sinned in that thing" (Leviticus 5:5). "True confession is always of a specific character, and acknowledges particular sins" (*Steps to Christ*, page 38). But how can we intelligently and honestly confess sins that we are not aware of?

For example, selfish motives are most certainly sin. One may behave and pray today in utter sincerity believing that he or she has acted unselfishly, and then tomorrow recognize that there was sinful selfishness of motive in that act or word of yesterday.

This does not mean that one was not converted yesterday; but if we resist and reject that further conviction of the Holy Spirit and refuse to repent, then indeed we lose the conversion we had yesterday. There is no way that we can misunderstand both Scripture and the Spirit of Prophecy by assuming that repentance is anything but a lifelong, ever deepening experience. Otherwise we lock ourselves into a terrible state of arrogant self-righteousness.

Does Ellen White speak of this idea of unknown sin being brought to our knowledge?

Yes, many times. We can briefly quote only a few examples:

Those who really desire to glorify God will be thankful for the exposure of every idol and every sin, that they may see these evils and put them away (*Testimonies for the Church*, vol. 4, page 354).

Everyone has undiscovered traits of character that must come to light through trials. God allows those who are self-sufficient to be sorely tempted, that they may understand their helplessness (ibid., vol. 7, page 211).

If we have defects of character of which we are not aware, [the Lord] gives us discipline that will bring those defects to our knowledge, that we may overcome them. … But nothing is revealed but that which was in you (*Review and Herald*, August 6, 1889).

God's law is the test of our actions. His eye sees every act, searches every chamber of the mind, detecting all lurking self-deception and all hypocrisy (*That I May Know Him*, page 290).

The work of restoration can never be thorough unless the roots of evil are reached. Again and again the shoots have been clipped, while the root of bitterness has been left to spring up and defile many; but the very depth of the hidden evil must be reached, the moral senses must be judged, and judged again, in the light of the divine presence (*Seventh-day Adventist Bible Commentary*, vol. 5, page 1152).

Many … are placed in circumstances that seem to call forth all the evil of their nature. Faults are revealed, of which they did not even suspect the existence. … [God] brings these persons into different positions and varied circumstances that they may discover in their character the defects which have been concealed from their own knowledge (*The Ministry of Healing*, pages 470, 471).

Is this not a discouraging idea?

Nothing that the Holy Spirit brings to our knowledge can be discouraging. He is the Comforter!

If one has a cancer that is soon to kill him, should he be discouraged if the doctor diagnosed it correctly and performed the necessary surgery that would save his life?

But how important is it to overcome unknown sin? Doesn't Jesus as our Substitute cover for it? Doesn't His robe of righteousness hide our unknown deformities of character?

The issue is not the salvation of our own poor little souls, but the honor and vindication of Christ. We ourselves may be blissfully ignorant of our unknown sin, but nevertheless it brings shame on Christ. It can even bring perplexity to others who can see our unchristlikeness that we cannot see. Youth are often discouraged by the sinful inconsistencies of their undiscerning elders.

It is true that if we die before the Holy Spirit has brought unknown sin to our knowledge, we can trust our Substitute to "cover" for us. Martin Luther died while drinking his beer, and not knowing how sinful was his anti-Semitism that later encouraged the evils of Nazism. But his case in the judgment will not be as difficult as ours would be if we sin knowingly against far greater light.

If the Holy Spirit has brought unknown sin to our knowledge and we have resisted His "office work" and refused to repent, we may indeed make it impossible for ourselves to be saved at last. Here is the focal point of the Day of Atonement ministry of our High Priest. Ellen White related this work of the Holy Spirit's probing deeply to reveal unknown sin with the Day of Atonement ministry of Christ:

> We are in the day of atonement, and we are to work in harmony with Christ's work of cleansing the sanctuary from the sins of the people. Let no man who desires to be found with the wedding garment on, resist our Lord in his office work (*Review and Herald*, January 21, 1890; see also January 28, February 4, 11, 18, 25, March 4, 11, 18, etc.).

The cleansing of the heavenly sanctuary includes a parallel work in the hearts of God's people on earth (*The Great Controversy*, pages 425, 623). Its purpose is to prepare a people for translation. They must at last meet the Lord face to face without tasting death (1 Thessalonians 4:15-17).

But "our God is a consuming fire" (Hebrews 12:29). If there is sin still buried in our heart when we come into His presence, that fire will have to "consume" it, and we shall perish with it. That is why the loving Holy Spirit wants to bring it to our attention today!

Does our 1888 history illustrate the problem of unknown sin in the hearts of Seventh-day Adventists?

Ellen White has said numerous times that the sin of those who rejected the 1888 message was of the same nature as the sin of the Jews who rejected Christ (for example, MS 2, 1890; *Testimonies to Ministers and Gospel Workers*, page 64; *Review and Herald*, April 11, 1893). Yet they "knew not" what spirit they were of, she says again (MS 24, 1892).

Apart from the specific grace of God we are by nature no better than they were. As we all partake of the sin of crucifying Christ (apart from God's forgiveness received), so we partake of the guilt of our brethren of a century ago. Repentance is incumbent on us all.

Corporate repentance is repenting individually of sins which *but for the grace of God* we realize we would have committed if we had the opportunity. Dr. Arnold Wallenkampf says that what led our brethren in 1888 to reject the message was the sin of following others in "group dynamics" or "groupthink" (*What Every Adventist Should Know About 1888*, pages 45, 46).

Today, likewise, nothing but the choice to be crucified with Christ will save us from the sin of following "group dynamics" in the numerous challenges that today confront us. There is no way any of us can follow Christ except to be crucified with Him.

NOTES

QUESTIONS ABOUT CORPORATE AND DENOMINATIONAL REPENTANCE

What is the difference between "corporate confession" and "corporate repentance"?

"Corporate repentance" is a million miles away from a mere committee action, or a four-color advertisement promoting it as the latest "groupthink" strategy. That would never help, for there are many who because of ingrained "loyalty" will jump on any new program that is promoted by "groupthink," for they want to be "in" and thought well of. A "corporate confession" would accomplish nothing. As we near the end of time, the Lord cannot be satisfied with such a superficial work.

The word "corporate" has nothing to do with the organization of the hierarchy. Repentance is a gift of the Holy Spirit, not a constituency vote. The work of repentance is always individual and personal, but the word "corporate" is simply the proper term to describe how each "member of the body" relates to the Head and to one another (1 Corinthians 12 and Ephesians 4).

Corporate repentance is personally repenting of the sins of others as though they were our own, feeling the pain and guilt of other members of the body, which we realize would be ours but for the grace of Christ.

This is how the "message of Christ's righteousness" becomes relevant. His righteousness must be imputed 100 percent, for we do not have even 1 percent of our own. We share the corporate guilt of the whole world—but for the grace of Christ. No one of us is innately better than another. As Luther said, we are all made of the same dough. Every lion in Africa is by nature a man-eater, but few get "the opportunity" to eat human beings. We can say that lions share a corporate nature.

The Lord Jesus calls upon "the angel of the church of the Laodiceans" to "be zealous therefore, and repent" (Revelation 3:14, 19). While such repentance is always personal, it is also "of the body," and therefore "corporate."

The repentance of ancient Nineveh at the preaching of Jonah is an example of national repentance, led by "the king and his nobles" (Jonah 3:5-9). A repentance of the church today as a body would be denominational. The Lord will give the gift, and His honor requires that He have a people who respond, both leaders and laity (cf. Zechariah 12:10-13:1).

How can such a repentance ever pervade the body of the church?

Is the Seventh-day Adventist Church the true "remnant church" of Revelation 12:17? Is it the "Israel" of today? We believe the answer is yes.

Abraham's descendants were to be the "remnant church" of their day. They were to be God's vehicle for evangelizing the world. At that time He had true followers in all nations, just as He has true believers everywhere today (including for example, Islam, Buddhism, and Hinduism).

So why did God choose Abraham and his children as His visible "body" on earth? "In thee shall all families of the earth be blessed" (Genesis 12:3). In a great degree the history of his descendants became a disaster, but something is to happen in the end of time that has never happened before—the cleansing of the heavenly sanctuary. That grand purpose of God must be fulfilled in His people. This is why this church exists.

Scripture requires a denominated, visible church to be Christ's "body" on earth, not a scattered, disorganized mélange. A stomach here and an eye there and an ear far off do not constitute a "body." A "body" is a coordinated, united organism obedient to the head.

Will such a repentance ever pervade the body of the church?

Some critics and offshoots say, "No! Impossible." And it seems that others also say No, but for a different reason—they say it's not necessary. *But Jesus calls for it.* And His word cannot return unto Him void. We must remember that there is one personality who firmly opposes denominational repentance and who believes it is impossible. His name? Satan. Human wisdom is insufficient to answer the question. But the Bible assures us that such a repentance as a gift from God will indeed pervade the body of God's people, and Satan will be proven wrong:

... I will pour upon the house of David [the leadership] and upon the inhabitants of Jerusalem [the members] the spirit of grace and of supplications: and they shall look upon me whom they have pierced, and they shall mourn for him. ... In that day there shall be a fountain opened to the house of David and to the inhabitants of Jerusalem for sin and for uncleanness (Zechariah 12:10-13:1).

Further, Revelation pictures the church as finally overcoming (3:20, 21; 19:6-9). And Ellen White many times expressed the firm confidence that the Seventh-day Adventist Church will eventually repent and come into line with God's program (cf. *Testimonies for the Church*, vol. 8, pp. 249-251; vol. 9, pp. 20, 126; *Selected Messages*, book 2, pp. 390, 397; *Testimonies to Ministers and Gospel Workers*, pp. 49, 57, 58, 410; *Medical Ministry*, pp. 184, 185).

To doubt this is to stand on the great enemy's side, for Satan is determined that such repentance must never be experienced by the remnant church.

What can the Lord do to arouse His lukewarm, complacent, worldly people?

The 1888 history and message are to the Seventh-day Adventist Church what Calvary and the New Testament are to the Jews. Most Jews are like us, occupied with "just keeping their personal lives together," who couldn't care less what happened nearly 2000 years ago in their history, just as "we" (in general) think we can't care less what happened 100 years ago in our history.

But the 1888 message was the "beginning" of the latter rain and the loud cry of Revelation 18, just as Jesus of Nazareth was the Jews' Messiah. It was the Lord's purpose to make the Jewish nation His evangelists to the world at that time. It was the Lord's purpose in 1888 to infuse every Seventh-day Adventist congregation with the warmth of genuine *agape* love, to make them "foremost in uplifting Christ before the world."

Inspired testimony tells us that we blew it "just like the Jews." Ellen White tells the naked truth. The century-old by-products of that rejection of truth are the terrible lukewarmness, legalism, criticism, confusion, and disunity seen almost everywhere. The beautiful message of Christ's much more abounding grace has "in a great degree" been kept away from our people and from the world itself (*Selected Messages*, book 1, pages 234, 235).

Critics and legalists can have a field day decrying how "sin [has] abounded" within the church, but what is most important is how "grace did much more abound." The Lord can do for us what He longed to do for the Jews—to give the gift of repentance. And in this time of the cleansing of the sanctuary His people must overcome where the ancient Jews failed.

Do our scholars and General Conference leaders approve of the message of corporate and denominational repentance? If many oppose it, should it be proclaimed?

If we are doubtful and perplexed, it would be well to ask the Lord this question. He invites us, "Come now, and let us reason together, saith the Lord" (Isaiah 1:18). Surely He will not despise the earnest and sincere prayer of His people. Says David, "He inclined unto me, and heard my cry" (Psalm 40:1).

We do know that sometimes the Lord commissions people to say something that official leadership does not want them to say. Discussing in context the 1888 experience, Ellen White refers to the experience of the apostles and says:

"The angel of the Lord by night opened the prison doors, and brought them forth, and said, Go, stand and speak in the temple to the people all the words of this life." We see here that the men in authority are not always to be obeyed, even though they may profess to be teachers of Bible doctrine. There are many today who feel indignant and aggrieved that any voice should be raised presenting ideas that differ from their own in regard to points of religious belief. …

But we see that the God of heaven sometimes commissions men to teach that which is regarded as contrary to the established doctrines. …The Holy Spirit will, from time to time, reveal the truth through its own chosen agencies, and no man, not even a priest or ruler, has a right to say, You shall not give publicity to your opinions, because I do not believe them. That wonderful "I" may attempt to put down the Holy Spirit's teaching. Men may for a time attempt to smother it and kill it, but that will not make error truth, or truth error (*Testimonies to Ministers and Gospel Workers*, pages 69, 70).

Note the word "sometimes." A true follower of Christ will respect divinely appointed authority. David would not lift his hand against King Saul, "the Lord's anointed," even though Saul was clearly apostate. Elijah was loyal and respectful toward King Ahab, although honest with him, too. Jeremiah respected Kings Jehoikim and Zedekiah, although they were also apostate, and tried in loyalty to help them.

At His trial, Jesus spoke kindly and straightforwardly to the officer who slapped Him in the face, and Paul once apologized to the high priest. That "sometimes" should humble anyone who imagines on his own that he is commissioned by the Lord to a special work. Like Gideon, he should put out the fleece time and again, to be sure he is not running ahead of the angel's leading. An intelligent, informed person will be extremely careful and prayerful before saying anything publicly that leadership does not want him or her to say! But that "sometimes" has definitely applied to Seventh-day Adventist history:

Even Seventh-day Adventists are in danger of closing their eyes to truth as it is in Jesus, because it contradicts something which they have taken for granted as truth but which the Holy Spirit teaches is not truth. ...

Finite men should beware of seeking to control their fellow men, taking the place assigned to the Holy Spirit. Let not men feel that it is their prerogative to give to the world what they suppose to be truth, and refuse that anything should be given contrary to their ideas. ...

That men should keep alive the spirit that ran riot at Minneapolis [1888] is an offense to God (ibid., pages 70-76; May 30, 1896).

The Lord is leading a people, not just a few individuals. It is easy for zealous souls to imagine that they have a commission from the Lord to say something when it may not be true. Jeremiah warned against people running when the Lord had not sent them (23:21-32). Nevertheless, our history warns us that we must not blindly follow leadership in opposition to the Holy Spirit's clear direction. Says Ellen White:

Some of our leading brethren have frequently taken their position on the wrong side; and if God would send a message and wait for these older brethren to open the way for its advancement, it would never reach the people (*Gospel Workers*, page 303).

117

It is only reasonable to inquire if perchance we are today acting out the 1888 history all over again. The presumptive evidence in principle would indicate that the sad history *must be repeated unless denominational repentance has taken place.* It is a common axiom that a nation that does not know its history is fated to repeat it. The same applies to a church. But leadership can change. Lessons can be learned.

Day by day we are sealing our eternal destiny by how we react to the Holy Spirit's leading. Knowing our history, if we choose to repeat it, we will surely judge ourselves as unworthy of eternal life. God forgave the Jewish nation for crucifying Christ. He did not forgive them when they repeated that sin in rejecting the apostles and stoning Stephen.

The important question to ask is: Does the Lord Jesus Christ Himself call the leadership of the church to repentance? The answer is found in Revelation 3:19 where the call to "repent" is addressed "unto the angel of the church of the Laodiceans." If this call is valid, conscientious people among the "house of David and the inhabitants of Jerusalem" will recognize it and fearlessly echo it.

There are evidences that indicate some growing acceptance in leadership of the essential elements of the 1888 message. A former General Conference president firmly supported the 1888 presentation of justification in his Week of Prayer reading for November, 1988. Dr. Wallenkampf's book on justification (*Review and Herald*, chapter 5) also takes the same position. And his book on the 1888 history is thoroughly in accord with Ellen White's writings on the subject. These are very encouraging signs!

If a massive glacier can be pried loose even an inch or two, an avalanche might follow.

In 1988 the church celebrated the Centennial year. Now are these issues dying a natural death? Can we now forget 1888 as we face the future?

Considerable progress toward reality marked the 1988 Centennial. Now the candid judgment is almost universally recognized that not only was the 1888 message the beginning of the latter rain and the loud cry, but leadership were on the wrong side of the issues. This about-face is a phenomenal development in Seventh-day Adventist history.

It has also been said that it is virtually impossible ever to achieve denominational unity on the 1888 issues. But the speed with which the history issue has now been turned upside down and resolved with virtual unanimity gives encouragement to believe that the remaining issues of disagreement may also be resolved much sooner than we think.

One main issue now remains: *what was the authentic 1888 message?* The Holy Spirit will not permit us to evade the duty of recovering it.

Is the message in process of being recovered?

It should not take long to determine objectively what the message was. Jones and Waggoner's published writings are readily available. It is impossible to misconstrue their meaning.

A growing segment of church members have already caught a glimpse of what the message is, either by reading newly published reprints of the 1888 messengers' works, or seeing slides on the screen in 1888 message seminars and conferences.

A nearly universal testimony from those who have attended indicates that the message comes across as refreshingly different. "I never before understood the gospel so clearly." "We have never heard these things preached before." "Why has no one ever told us?"

A century ago Ellen White declared that "there is not one in one hundred who understands for himself the Bible truth on this subject [the 1888 idea of justification by faith] … The people have not an intelligent faith" (*Review and Herald*, Sept. 3,1889). "Our churches are dying for the want of teaching on the subject of righteousness by faith in Christ, and on kindred truths" (*Review and Herald*, March 25, 1890). When the reality of the 1888 message is understood, it becomes apparent that Ellen White's 1889 comments are still present truth today. Extremely few have understood the message.

But there is heartening good news. While denominational pride is humbled, confidence in the Seventh-day Adventist mission and its accomplishment is renewed.

On all levels of the church we see a revival of "historic Adventism." Is this the same as the 1888 message?

The 1888 message is not a mere revival of "historic Adventism," nor is it a new legalism. Those who rejected the message at Minneapolis a century ago were all "historic Adventists." If we could resurrect our most dynamic preachers of 50 or 60 years ago who were also "historic Adventists," their preaching would wither in the merciless light that now shines in these last days. It was their preaching that prepared the way for our present state of confusion and pluralism, for it was largely devoid of the unique 1888 Good News concepts.

The reason is that they were largely uninformed of the actual realities of the 1888 message. Due to the failures of Jones and Waggoner, deep prejudice against their message permeated the church in the years after Ellen White's death (1915). The prevailing concepts of the gospel in the decades that followed were conditioned by the "Victorious Life" enthusiasm which infiltrated Adventism in the 1920s and 1930s. Our denominational leaders of that era publicly embraced these Evangelical ideas which had their source in the *Sunday School Times*, mistakenly assuming that they were the same as the 1888 message.

The "Victorious Life" sounds good. What was that message?

"Victory over sin" was the theme, inspiring hope and confidence that the message would prepare a people for the coming of the Lord. It was an especially appealing doctrine in the bewildering post-World War I era of the 1920s. But the "how" of the doctrine left an aching void.

Sincerely unaware of the unique truths of the 1888 message, our leading brethren of that era were powerless to distinguish between the genuine and the counterfeit. The question that now demands attention is whether at any time since the 1930s have we recovered the missing spiritual nutriments of the 1888 message.

The "Victorious Life" was the same message proclaimed by Evangelicals in the 1910s and 1920s. Its purpose was to instill a confidence that one is saved apart from obedience to all the commandments of God. It was ecumenical in spirit, sharing the essential concepts of the "inner life" devotional movement that has flourished in the Roman Catholic Church in modern times.

The most poignant loss is often that which is unrealized. This is the point of Christ's appeal to Laodicea: "Thou knowest not" that something precious has been lost (Revelation 3:15-18). Ezekiel records the tragic fact that the priests serving in Solomon's temple in the days of Zedekiah did not know when the presence of the Lord was absent from the temple (chapters 8-10).

The message of the three angels without the message of the fourth angel is not sufficient to lighten the earth with glory. And when history demands a response to God's opening providences, as in 1888, and God's people react negatively, the resulting ferment spawns innumerable wrongs. This is the story of thousands of years of history. It is also the spiritual tragedy of our past century of history.

NOTES

QUESTIONS ABOUT THE MESSAGE AND CHURCH ORGANIZATION

Are the 1888 publications intended to function in competition with denominational books and periodicals?

No. We continually urge people to be well informed by reading the *Adventist Review* and our denominational literature, as well as other literature published by loyal Seventh-day Adventists which presents information not available in official publications. We are presenting a message that they do not present, seeking to meet a need that they are not meeting.

Does the 1888 message attract fanatics, legalists, and critics?

Those most interested in the message are not "theologians" or "religious hobbyists who are looking for a cause," as some assume. It is true that some fanatics try to capitalize on the interest and infiltrate refined legalism. Few will dare to say outright that they reject the 1888 message.

Uncharitable critics seize upon the undeniable facts of our history in order to condemn leadership. But these are certainly not interested in the much more abounding grace of the 1888 message itself, and do not appreciate its import.

In fact, ultra-right wing "conservatives" are sometimes vociferous in condemning its basic essentials. There were "certain [who] came from James" to trouble the Galatians with their "Christian" legalism (Galatians 2:12). Those whose hearts welcome the 1888 message are humble lay-members looking for meaning in Adventism, plus pastors and administrators seeking the blessing of the Holy Spirit.

And many youth yearn for a Christ who is "nigh at hand" and not "afar off" who can save *from*, not *in*, sin. The enemy of righteousness tried to bring in fanaticism a century ago, but Ellen White likened the revivals from 1888-1891 to the Midnight Cry of 1844 where she said fanaticism disappeared like frost before the morning sun.

Unfortunately confusion entered in after the 1893 General Conference Session. When the people finally realized how strong was opposition to the message, they were perplexed and confused and did not know what to do. Only then was some fanaticism able to get in. Wholehearted support from the General Conference would have brought the kind of unity that would have kept fanaticism out. Again in our day, wholehearted, united acceptance of the message of Christ's righteousness will stifle fanaticism in the bud. The gospel will never produce fanaticism; opposition to it will.

Did Ellen White oppose or support "irregular" ministries?

Contrary to the wishes of some conference officials, she said, "Brethren Sutherland and Magan should be encouraged to solicit means for the support of their work" (*Special Testimonies*, Series B, No. 11, pages 10, 17, 19-21, 36). "There should be many at work in what are called 'irregular lines.' If one hundred workers would step out of the 'regular lines,' and take up self-sacrificing work, … souls would be won to the Lord" (Letter J109, 1901).

Should all publishing in this country be confined to the Review and Herald and Pacific Press?

While strongly supporting the organization of the church as the Lord has led in establishing it, Crisler quoted Ellen White at length in support of independent ministries that the Lord unexpectedly moves upon people to initiate. She wrote as follows, he says, "to a conference president in the South who looked upon self-supporting missionary work as something irregular":

> Christ accepts and communes with the most lowly. He does not accept men because of their capabilities or eloquence, but because they seek His face, desiring His help. His Spirit, moving upon the heart, arouses every faculty to vigorous action. In these unpretentious ones the Lord sees the most

precious material, which will stand the storm and tempest, heat and pressure. God sees not as man sees. He judges not from appearance. He searches the heart and judgeth righteously.

Who has sent you to a field where a good work has been done, to show your zeal by tearing it to pieces? Is this working in the regular lines? If so, it is high time that we worked in irregular lines. God is displeased with your work.

There are men who will spend and be spent to win souls. In obedience to the great commission, many will go forth to work for the Master. Under the ministration of angels, common men will be moved upon by the Spirit of God and led to warn people in the highways and byways. They are to be strengthened and encouraged and as fast as possible prepared for labor, that success may crown their efforts. They harmonize with unseen, heavenly instrumentalities. They are workers together with God, and their brethren should bid them Godspeed and pray for them as they labor in Christ's name.

No one is authorized to hinder such workers. They should be treated with the greatest respect. No one should speak a taunting word to them, as in the rough places of the earth they sow the gospel seed.

Christ will be with these workers. The angels of heaven will respond to the self-sacrificing efforts put forth. By the power of the Holy Spirit Jesus will move upon hearts. God will work miracles in the conversion of sinners. The workers will be filled with joy as they see souls converted. Men and women will be gathered into church fellowship. ... Their persevering prayers will bring souls to the cross. ...

Brother _____ , there should be many at work in the lines which in your judgment you call "irregular lines." Do you think that your criticisms are the production of the Holy Spirit? ... (pages 12-14).

Ellen White could have had the Pacific Press or the Review and Herald publish her *Steps to Christ*. In fact, she had a non-Adventist publisher produce it in 1892.

But in these quotations, Ellen White is speaking of self-supporting evangelistic work among non-Adventists.

It was God's plan that the 1888 message of Christ's righteousness should go both to the church and to the world (*Testimonies to Ministers and Gospel Workers*, pages 91-93; *Selected Messages*, book 1, pages 234, 235). Revival, reformation, and repentance are essential to the church *before* the light of the fourth angel can shine clearly to the world at large.

Therefore a message of much more abounding grace which Ellen White declared to be the "beginning" of the latter rain must, in the providence of God, be brought to the church first. Such work is the purest soul-winning evangelism.

In the meantime, this message wins back church members who have become discouraged and wandered away, and also wins non-Adventists. The administrators of the church can rejoice at the new converts, reclaimed members, and increase of tithe returned to the church treasury as the result of a revival of the 1888 message.

Crisler quotes another letter which Ellen White wrote "to a General Conference leader" in 1901:

> So often the same old difficulties arise and are presented in regard to disturbing the "regular lines." ... How many more years will it be before our brethren receive the clear, keen perception which calls evil evil and good good? When will men cease to depend upon the same routine which has left so much work undone, so many fields unworked? Is not the present presentation enough to make men see that a revival is necessary and a reformation essential? If not, it is useless for me to repeat the same things over and over again. ... If we can get away from the regular lines into something which, though irregular, is after God's order, it may cut away something of the irregular working which has led away from Bible principles.
>
> God's principles are the only safe principles for us to follow. Phariseeism was filled with regular lines, but so perverted were the principles of justice that God declared, "Judgment is turned away backward and equity can not enter; yea, truth faileth, and he that departeth from evil maketh himself a prey." How true these words have proved! ... It is as hard today to break away from the regular lines as it was in Christ's day (pages 15, 16).

Is it possible that the Holy Spirit has Himself moved upon the hearts of men and women and youth to support and proclaim the 1888 message of Christ's righteousness?

We would not dare to say that it is impossible for the Holy Spirit to do so. Neither should anyone proudly or arrogantly claim that he is being led by the Holy Spirit. "Let him that thinketh he standeth take heed lest he fall." In the closing days of earth's history, each child of God must walk humbly with the Lord, seeking His guidance at every step.

Clarence Crisler summarizes Ellen White's counsel "in a letter addressed to the president of the General Conference in 1901," saying:

> The principle is set forth that when the appointed agencies in the church fail to do a work which must be done by some means, it is in harmony with the will of God that such work be undertaken by individuals impressed by the Holy Spirit to do this work (page 16).

Principles are eternal. Applications of those principles depend on circumstances. For sure, we know that the Holy Spirit is very much alive today and that He is working through many agencies in order to bring revival, reformation, and repentance to the Seventh-day Adventist Church and to prepare the church to enlighten the world.

It is incumbent on each member of the church to make certain he or she cooperates with the Holy Spirit, and does not oppose Him as did our leadership a hundred years ago. They were inclined to do so again at the time Ellen White at the beginning of this century penned her earnest appeals regarding the failure of "the regular lines."

We must also take note of counsel that Clarence Crister said she gave against "rash moves and ... independence of spirit" (page 17). The Lord is not leading one or two only; He is leading a world church.

The work of "Elijah" for today will not be limited to one or two individuals striking out on their own without seeking counsel from other responsible workers. All who would work must counsel with those who have an intelligent understanding of what needs to be done. Never has it been more important that each one be distrustful of self, and seek earnestly again and again for counsel to know for sure what his or her duty is. "All ye are brethren," the Lord says.

Is there a need for the 1888 message that outweighs the opposition to it?

The world itself is in a frightful condition. Any newspaper or newscast can remind us. The terrible problems that afflict Africa, Central and South America, the Middle East, the Soviet Union, the Far East, India, the U.S. etc., are the result of a vast famine for hearing the word of the Lord, the pure gospel of Christ as "the third angel's message in verity."

Although there are many devoted men and women in its leadership and membership, the Roman Catholic Church is not presenting that pure message. Neither are the Protestant churches or the Evangelicals, sincere and consecrated as they may be.

Neither is the pre-1888 or non-1888 understanding of the "third angel's message" clear enough to lighten the earth with the glory of the fourth angel of Revelation 18. We would be recreant to our duty, undeserving of the air we breathe by the grace of God, were we not to do our best to support the message that inspiration has designated as its "beginning."

The Lord entrusted that message to Seventh-day Adventists over a century ago and "commanded" that it go to the world. Repentance, revival, and reformation within the church are our present need, in order that we may be prepared to sound the message clearly to the world itself. The proclamation of the gospel is always a constructive work, upbuilding, joyous, unifying, and healing in its influence.

The "28 Fundamental Beliefs" voted in a General Conference Session as our virtual "creed" say nothing about the 1888 message. They are neutral on the nature of Christ and "righteousness by faith in an end-time setting." What place then has the 1888 message?

Some have earnestly contended that since the 1888 message is "highly controversial" and has never been accepted by the official leadership of the church, it should not be presented to the church or to the world.

It is of course very true, and openly acknowledged by present leadership, that the message was indeed not accepted by the official leadership of the church a century ago. We can add that at no time since has it been accepted. In particular, three of its most essential elements are now singled out as so "highly controversial" that silence on them is actually enjoined: (1) "The human nature of Christ;" (2) "the nature of sin;" and (3) "righteousness by faith in an end-time setting" (*An Appeal for Unity*, 1989, General Conference, page 5).

Is nothing to be preached that is not articulated in the "28 Fundamental Beliefs"? The "28" say not a word about prayer; should we therefore not preach about it?

It may be said that to preach about prayer is permissible even though it is not one of the 28 articles, because it is not "controversial," and Ellen White does support it in her *Steps to Christ* chapter, "The Privilege of Prayer." But Ellen White possibly says more about the 1888 message (1812 pages) than she does about prayer! She says that God "commanded" expressly that the 1888 message should be "given to the world" (*Testimonies to Ministers and Gospel Workers*, page 92).

Experience for some years indicates that when the authentic 1888 message is permitted to be presented, "controversy" becomes virtually nil. A sober, solemn realization that the message is Bible truth pervades congregations who come to hear and who see the message on the screen. It dispels opposition.

But even if at rare times some wish to counter the message with controversy, we are told that in God's providence this should not be taken as an excuse to silence the message. Speaking directly in context about the 1888 message, Ellen White says:

> The fact that there is no controversy or agitation among God's people should not be regarded as conclusive evidence that they are holding fast to sound doctrine. There is reason to fear that they may not be clearly discriminating between truth and error. When no new questions are started by investigation of the Scriptures, when no difference of opinion arises which will set men [and women] to searching the Bible for themselves, to make sure that they have the truth, there will be many now, as in ancient times, who will hold to tradition, and worship they know not what. ...
>
> Our brethren should be willing to investigate in a candid way every point of controversy. ... We should never permit the spirit to be manifested that arraigned the priests and rulers against the Redeemer of the world. They complained that He disturbed the people, and they wished He would let

them alone; for He caused perplexity and dissension (*Gospel Workers*, pages 298-302).

The brethren of the General Conference and the *Review* of a century ago rejected the message because they thought it was not included in what they *assumed* were their "fundamental beliefs." Ellen White rebuked them, declaring that the 1888 message "is the third angel's message in verity" (*Review and Herald*, April 1, 1890). If that message is what she said it was, "the beginning" of the loud cry of Revelation 18, it follows logically that it is still today the "28 Fundamental Beliefs" in verity.

Why do you believe that the Seventh-day Adventist Church will never become Babylon?

The Seventh-day Adventist Church *will* overcome, *will* repent, *will* refuse to accept the mark of the beast, because the honor and vindication of Christ require that His "body" respond to Him. And Revelation says that "His Bride" must make "herself ready" for it to be true that the "marriage of the Lamb is come" (19:6, 7).

It is true that in all past history God's organized people have often failed. The Jews were cast off, and the Christian church through history has gone into apostasy, and this church at present faces serious problems. But that does not "guarantee" that she will fail in the end.

The ultimate issue is not the salvation of our own little souls, but the honor and vindication of the Son of God, who gave His blood to save the church. He did not die in vain; He will see of the travail of His soul and be satisfied.

That does not mean that everyone in the church or its leadership will automatically overcome; there will be a great shaking, and judgments will come. Where we may see only floors of rich grain, the judgment will reveal there is only chaff (*Testimonies for the Church*, vol. 5, page 81). But there will be some good grain!

There is abundant evidence in Scripture and in Ellen White's writings that those who are at last shaken out of the church will be the disloyal ones. Inspired evidence does not indicate that the loyal ones will be shaken out (cf. Isaiah 17:6, 7).

What makes the difference is the cleansing of the sanctuary— something that has never happened in all previous history. This includes imparting to God's people a new motivation never fully embraced by His corporate church in previous history—a concern for

Christ as a bride feels a concern for her bridegroom. This will not be a mere concern for self.

It is very true that without that refreshingly different motivation, it will be impossible for her to overcome, or for any corporate body to overcome. Hence, the need for a "final atonement," a final reconciliation with Christ; and this involves the 1888 message of Christ's righteousness. Otherwise that truly Christ-centered motivation can never prevail. Mere concern for personal security will never prepare a people to meet the test of the mark of the beast.

How can our present leadership repent for something done over 100 years ago by the then leaders?

We must remember that repentance is a gift which the Lord gives, not something we can initiate ourselves (Acts 5:31). Our Lord calls to "the angel of the church of the Laodiceans" to repent (Revelation 3:19). Surely when we have faith His biddings become enablings. Thus there has to be a way in which His call can be responded to.

Since repentance is a gift of the Holy Spirit, we must leave Him to bring the experience to His people in His own way. What is important is that we get out of His way and let Him impart the gift. The widespread doubt that He will give the gift is hindering Him.

The basic heart of God's people is honest; when they know the truth, they will respond. The publication of the four volumes of *The Ellen G. White 1888 Materials* is a step in the right direction. At last she is permitted to speak without hindrance. Further, the frank acknowledgements of the truth of the 1888 history in Dr. Robert Olson's article in the February 1988 *Ministry* magazine is the first time in decades that this has been openly and frankly published. The Lord will begin to work. We are indeed facing the final events in the great controversy.

Is it possible that sinful human beings like ourselves can have a part in vindicating Christ in the final crisis?

"We" can bring dishonor upon Him:

Reveal Christ as He is. … O how His glory is dimmed by His professed followers because they are earthly-minded, disobedient, unthankful, and unholy! How shamefully is the

Lord Jesus kept in the background! How is His mercy, His forbearance, His longsuffering, and His matchless love veiled, and His honor beclouded by the perversity of His followers! (*That I May Know Him*, page 345).

If God's people can bring *dishonor* upon Him, would it not follow that by receiving His gift of repentance, they can bring *honor* upon Him?

Then the end will come. God will vindicate His law [not only *has* vindicated it] and deliver His people. … When the great controversy shall be ended … the plan of redemption having been completed, the character of God is revealed to all created intelligences. … Then the extermination of sin will vindicate God's love and establish His honor before a universe of beings (*The Desire of Ages*, pages 763, 764).

Although the cross did indeed "vindicate" God's law and reveal His character, that vindication and revelation will not be complete until the end of the controversy.

The Bible makes clear that in the end, God's people will share with Christ the privilege of defeating Satan in the great controversy:

… They overcame him [Satan] by the blood of the Lamb, and by the word of their testimony … (Revelation 12:11).

In Him we were also chosen, having been predestined according to the plan of Him who works out everything in conformity with the purpose of His will, in order that we, who were the first to hope in Christ, might be for the praise of His glory (Ephesians 1:11, 12, *New International Version* [NIV]).

His intent was that now, through the church, the manifold wisdom of God should be made known to the rulers and authorities in the heavenly realms (Ephesians 3:10, NIV).

How can the church do this?

There is an answer:

The church being endowed with the righteousness of Christ is His depository, in which the wealth of His mercy, His love, His grace, is to appear in full and final display. … In their untainted purity and spotless perfection Christ looks upon His people as the reward of all His sufferings, His humiliation, and His love, and the supplement of His glory (*General Conference Bulletin*, 1893, page 409).

The church is the repository of the riches of the grace of Christ; and through the church will eventually be made manifest, even to the principalities and powers in heavenly places, the final and full display of the love of God (*The Youth's Instructor*, July 13, 1893).

Although the cross was a perfect "display of the love of God," yet something further is needed before that "display" is "final and full." Although it was complete at the cross, according to 1 John 4:12, in some important way His love is also to be "perfected in us."

The Lord has sent to our world a message of warning, even the three angels' messages. All heaven is waiting to hear us vindicate God's law, declaring it to be holy, just, and good. Where are those who will do this work? (*Review and Herald*, April 16, 1901).

What does it mean to "vindicate the law"?

"This character Christ represented by living that law, thus vindicating it" (*Review and Herald*, January 23, 1900). His people also have an important role to fill. God's people are not like ants on a log floating down a river with nothing to do but passively ride along. God honors them with responsibility:

The Saviour came to glorify the Father by the demonstration of His love; so the Spirit was to glorify Christ by revealing His grace to the world. The very image of Christ is to be reproduced in humanity. The honor of God, the honor of Christ, is involved in the perfection of the character of His people (*The Desire of Ages*, page 671).

Satan stands by to taunt Christ and His angels with insults, saying, "I have them! I have them! I have prepared my deception for them. Your blood is worthless here. Your intercessions and power and wonderful works may as well cease; I have them! They are mine!" (*Testimonies for the Church*, vol. 2, page 143).

Note that Satan specifically charges that the sacrifice of Christ is "worthless" so long as God's people fail to demonstrate its efficacy. "To disprove Satan's claim is the work of Christ and of all who bear His name" (*Education*, page 154). "If they [God's people] ... should prove unworthy, and lose their lives because of their own defects of character, then God's holy name would be reproached" (*The Great Controversy*, page 619).

"The reproach of His disciple's sin is cast upon Christ. It causes Satan to triumph" (ibid., page 811). "Our Lord is put to shame by those who claim to serve Him, but who misrepresent His character" (*The Desire of Ages*, pages 438, 439). If they can "reproach His name," can they not also vindicate His name?

Suppose that all of God's people should fail in the final crisis. Would this cause Satan to "triumph"?

"The church, in His name, is to carry to glorious perfection the work which He has commenced" (*Seventh-day Adventist Bible Commentary*, vol. 5, page 1146).

The Lord Jesus Christ came to dispute the usurpation of Satan in the kingdom of this world. *The conflict is not yet ended*; and as we draw near the close of time, the battle waxes more intense ... *Christ will be represented in the person of those who accept the truth*, and who identify their interest with that of their Lord [as a Bride for her husband] (ibid., pages 1105, 1106; emphasis added; see also *Signs of the Times*, September 7, 1891).

Before the ship reaches its safe harbor we can be sure that fearful storms will buffet her. But the Captain is in charge. He will not entrust His vessel to those who would only destroy her. The News from heaven *is Good*.

Let's believe it!

SELECTIONS FROM THE ELLEN G. WHITE 1888 MATERIALS

Paging references are to the four volumes of
The Ellen G. White 1888 Materials

The statements reproduced here contain her explicit endorsements of the message of Jones and Waggoner. There are many more that are implicit in the four volumes and in some *Review* articles. In reading through this material one has a sense of *déjà vu;* as a church we are re-living this history all over again more than a century later. The same unfair criticism of Jones and Waggoner and their message has featured prominently in our current denominational publications. In her day, Ellen White was heartsick to see us repeating the history of the Jews. What would she say today to see us repeat it again?

VOLUME ONE

Dr. Waggoner has opened to you precious light, not new, but old light which has been lost sight of by many minds, and is now shining forth in clear rays (page 175).

… these men whom God has appointed to do a special work in His cause (page 186).

… We have had to work and pray and work even to have Brother Jones obtain a hearing in Battle Creek (page 189).

Brother A. T. Jones spoke to the people, also Brother E. J. Waggoner, and the people heard many precious things that would be to them a comfort and a strength to their faith (pages 205-206).

… The Lord has raised up men and given them a solemn message to bear to His people (page 210).

Elder E. J. Waggoner had the privilege ... of presenting his views upon justification by faith and the righteousness of Christ in relation to the law. This was no new light, but it was old light placed where it should be in the third angel's message (page 211).

... I had heard precious truths uttered that I could respond to with all my heart, ... I felt inexpressibly grateful to God, for I knew it was the message for this time (page 217).

... a Christ-like spirit manifested, such as Elder E. J. Waggoner had shown all through the presentation of his views (page 219).

... men whom they and I had reason to respect (page 228).

... He has given these men [A. T. Jones and E. J. Waggoner] a work to do, and a message to bear which is present truth for this time, ... the very message that I know to be present truth for the people of God for this time (page 274).

... He has great light for us at this time (page 276).

... God had made these men messengers to give light and truth to the people (page 179).

Elder A. T. Jones has labored faithfully to instruct those assembled and in breaking to their souls the Bread of Life. ... The plan of salvation so clearly and simply defined (page 280).

... The plan of salvation ... has been made so clear that a child may understand (page 281).

If this message that has been preached here is not present truth for this time, I know not how we can determine what is truth (page 286).

Elder Jones and myself occupied the preaching hours, and the Lord imparted to the speakers His grace in rich measure (page 288).

I think that Elder A. T. Jones should attend our large camp meetings, and give to our people and to outsiders as well the precious subject of faith and the righteousness of Christ (page 291).

Brother Jones has patiently instructed the people (page 291).

… work was being carried to make of none effect the labors of Eld. A. T. Jones and my work (page 298).

… clear waters of the streams of Lebanon (page 305).

… the way my brethren treated the servants whom the Lord sent to them with messages of truth (page 317).

Brother A. T. Jones talked upon the subject of justification by faith, and many received it as light and truth (page 317).

… contempt for their brethren whom the Lord sent with a message to them (page 322).

… they have thought and said worse things of Brethren Jones and Waggoner (page 323).

… That which was light from heaven was resisted (page 334).

You place Elder Jones in a false position just as … others placed him in at Minneapolis (page 336).

What do you think of this light that these men are presenting? Why I have been presenting it to you for the last 45 years—the matchless charms of Christ. … When Brother Waggoner brought out these ideas in Minneapolis, it was the first clear teaching of this subject from any human lips I had heard, excepting the conversations between myself and my husband. … And when another presented it, every fiber of my heart said, Amen (page 349).

… their own incorrect version of the matter, which was unfavorable to Brethren A. T. Jones, E. J. Waggoner, W. C. White and myself (page 352).

Brother Jones will wait for an invitation from you. You should do your duty in regard to this matter and open the way before him (page 355).

… used all their powers to pick some flaws in the messengers and in the message, and they grieved the Spirit of God (page 368).

… It was not pleasant to fight every inch for any privileges and advantages to bring the truth before the people (page 379).

The Lord is speaking through His delegated messengers (page 398).

... continue to reject Christ in the person of His messengers (page 398).

You reject Christ in rejecting the message He sends (page 399).

God has sent messages of light to His people, ... those whom God has made channels of light (page 400).

God has sent you a message which He wishes you to receive—a message of light and hope and comfort for the people of God (page 404).

It is a grievous sin in the sight of God for them to place themselves between the people and the message that He would have come to them (page 406).

... go over the same ground of refusing the message of mercy as the Jews did in the time of Christ (page 406).

... the special work He is doing at this time to arouse a lukewarm, slumbering church (page 414).

... the message which the Lord sends, ... the light of heaven (page 415).

The Lord has been appealing to His people in warnings, in reproofs, in counsels; but their ears have been deaf to the words of Jesus. Some have said, "If this message that Brother A. T. Jones has been have not received it?" (page 416).

If Elder Smith or Elder Butler should reject the message of truth which the Lord has sent to the people at this time, would their unbelief make the message error? No. ... Men who have occupied leading positions feel at liberty to despise the message and the messenger (pages 418-419).

... It has nearly broken my heart to see those who ... reject the truth for this time. ... Some who ought to have been first to catch the heavenly inspiration of truth have been directly opposed to the message of God (page 420).

When the message of God meets with opposition He gives it additional force ... the message of truth (page 421).

... His chosen agents (page 422).

... His message and messengers (page 423).

... those whom God is using (page 443).

VOLUME TWO

Elder Jones presented the Bible evidence of justification by faith (page 463).

I attended the eight o'clock meeting in the side room of the tabernacle, conducted by Elder Jones. There were a large number present and he presented the subject of justification by faith in a plain, distinct manner, in such marked simplicity that no one need to be in darkness, unless he has in him a decided heart of unbelief, to resist the workings of the Spirit of God (page 465).

I fear many will go away from this meeting greatly in need of the very blessings that it is their privilege to receive, just now and notwithstanding the most precious light given upon the importance of thorough sanctification through the truth (page 467).

Judgment must not be passed hastily on any man. ... Some stand criticizing and passing judgment both upon the message and the messenger sent of God (page 499).

Those who will not accept the message the Lord sends will soon begin a tirade against it. They see evidence enough to balance the mind in the right direction but they are too proud to submit. They are not willing to say that which they decided was all wrong is right (page 499).

The light which God is giving to His people may be slighted, refused, rejected, but it is thus treated at great peril to men's souls. Brethren, God is working for us, and I feel deeply in earnest that not one ray of heaven-sent light may be regarded with indifference. God's communication to man is to be appreciated and cherished. If we do not appreciate the light of heaven, it will be our condemnation; our position will be similar to that of the Jews when they rejected the Lord of life and glory (page I heard the jesting, the sarcastic remarks in regard to the messengers and the message—that doctrine that differed from their ideas of truth; and I was told there was a witness in every room as the witness was in Belshazzar's palace at that festival (page 517).

Why do you pursue the course you do in keeping away from meetings where points of truth are investigated? If you have a position, present it in clear lines (page 528).

If you have truth, tell it; if your brethren have truth, be humble and honest before God and say it is truth (page 528).

If the ideas presented before the Ministerial Institute are erroneous, come to the front like men and present candidly your Bible evidence why you cannot see the point as they do. This is your duty ... Do not stand in the position you do as leaders in the Sabbath School and resisting the light or views and ideas presented by men whom I know to be agents whom the Lord is using. You (sic) making of none effect as far as you can their words and not coming yourself to the light like Christians come to the word to investigate it together with humble hearts, not to investigate the Bible to bring it to your ideas, but bring your ideas to the Bible. It is your duty to do this (page 529).

Come and learn just the ideas advanced (page 531).

I know there have been efforts—a contrary influence—to throw back the light, the light which God has been forcing in here upon us in regard to the righteousness of Christ; but if God has ever spoken by me, it is the truth, brethren (page 537).

You can close the door of your heart that the light which God has sent you for the last year-and-a half—or nearly that—shall not have its influence and its effect upon your life, nor be brought into your religious experience. This is what God sends His messengers for (page 538).

Our young men look at the older men that stand still as a stick and will not move to accept any new light that is brought in; that they will laugh and ridicule what these men say and what they do as of no consequence. Who carries the burden of that laugh, and of that contempt, I ask you? Who carries it? It is the very ones that have interposed themselves between the light that God has given, and it shall not go to the people who should have it (pages 540-541).

If you have interposed between the people and the light, get out of the way, or God will move you out of the way (page 541).

... that I might stand side by side with the messengers of God that I knew were His messengers, that I knew had a message for His people. I gave my message with them right in harmony with the very message they were bearing (page 542).

I have traveled from place to place, attending meetings where the message of the righteousness of Christ was preached. I considered it a privilege to stand by the side of my brethren [Jones and Waggoner] ... I saw that the power of God attended the message. ... God has set His hand to do this work. ... Everywhere the message led to the confession of sin, and to the putting away of iniquity. ... How long will those at the head of the work keep themselves aloof from the message of God? ... Suppose you blot out the testimony that has been going during these last two years [1890] proclaiming the righteousness of Christ, who can you point to as bringing out special light for the people? This message as it has been presented should go to every church. ... the heavenly credentials (page 545).

We have light pouring in on us, and for months we have been pleading that the people would come up and accept the light; and they do not know whether to do it or not (page 556).

I believe without a doubt that God has given precious truth at the right time to Brother Jones and Brother Waggoner. Do I place them as infallible? Do I say that they will not make a statement or have an idea that cannot be questioned or that cannot be in error? Do I say so? No, I do not say any such thing. Nor do I say that of any man in the world. But I do say God has sent light, and do be careful how you treat it (page 566).

We claim God has given us light in the right time. And now we should receive the truth of God—receive it as of heavenly origin (page 567).

Do not turn away from the messages that God sends, as you did at Minneapolis (page 571).

We have not a doubt but that the Lord was with Elder Waggoner as he spoke yesterday. We have not a doubt of that. I have not a doubt that the power of God in rich measure was hanging over us, and everything was light in the Lord to me yesterday afternoon in the ministers' meeting (page 607).

If we place ourselves in a position that we will not recognize the light God sends or His messages to us, then we are in danger of sinning against the Holy Ghost. Then for us to turn and see if we can find some little thing that is done that we can hang some of our doubts upon and begin to question! The question is, has God sent the truth? Has God raised up these men to proclaim the truth? I say, yes, God has sent men to bring us the truth that we should not have had unless God had sent somebody to bring it to us. God has let me have a light of what His Spirit is, and therefore I accept it, and I no more dare to lift my hand against these persons, because it would be against Jesus Christ, who is to be recognized in His messengers (page 608).

Now, I want you to be careful, every one of you, what position you take, whether you enshroud yourselves in the clouds of unbelief because you see imperfections; you see a word or a little item, perhaps, that may take place, and judge them from that (pages 608-609).

I am glad—yes, I am so thankful—that some are beginning to see that there is light for us (page 612).

God has shown me that He raised up men here to carry the truth to His people, and that this is the truth (page 614).

Yesterday E. J. Waggoner gave a most powerful discourse. I have heard from many who were present, and their testimony was unanimous that God spoke through him (page 617).

Elder Waggoner spoke very humbly (page 625).

Waggoner spoke well (page 628).

I sent word for Brother [Dan] Jones [General Conference Secretary] to invite Elder Waggoner to speak. There seemed to be a little reluctance, but finally he was invited and gave a most precious discourse on the message to the Laodicean church—just what was needed (page 629).

I say it is from beneath and not in harmony with the Spirit of God, or with the message He has given His servants to bear at the present time (pages 630-631).

Every such mind that is susceptible to unbelief and the say-so of this one and that one, and that works against the light and the evidences that have been presented since the Minneapolis meeting—I tell you, brethren, I am terribly afraid that they will fall at last (page 638).

When [God] manifests His power as He has manifested it, it is very nigh unto the sin of the Holy Ghost to disbelieve it (page 639).

God has shown me that He raised up men here to carry the truth to His people (page 640).

Brother Jones talked very plainly, yet tenderly in regard to their crediting hearsay and not, in brotherly love, taking the matter to the one talked about and asking him if the report were true (page 642).

God has raised up His messengers to do His work for this time. Some have turned from the message of the righteousness of Christ to criticize the men and their imperfections, because they do not speak the message of truth with all the grace and polish desirable. They have too much zeal, are too much in earnest, speak with too much positiveness. … Christ has registered all the hard, proud, sneering speeches spoken against His servants as against Himself.

… The light which will lighten the earth with its glory will be called a false light by those who refused to walk in its advancing glory … Messages bearing the divine credentials have been sent to God's people, … set forth among us with beauty and loveliness, to charm all whose hearts were not closed with prejudice (page 673).

If Underwood is still in his opposition state, at war in feelings against A. T. Jones and E. J. Waggoner, keep him east (page 688).

The result of this opposition has required the delivery of this matter the more earnestly and decidedly, causing deeper searching into the subject and calling out an array of arguments that the messenger himself did not know was so firm, so full, so thorough upon this subject of justification by faith and the righteousness of Christ as our only hope (page 703).

The men who ought to have stood in the light, their voices heard on the right side of the question, were exercised on the wrong side to oppose that which was of God and resist that message which the Lord sends (page 703).

Elders Millers both presented your case as evidence that they should resist the Spirit of God, the message and the messenger. Bro. Rupert has a work of confession [to do] (page 733).

You responded to my letter of appeal by writing me a letter accusing Elder Jones of tearing up the pillars of our faith. Was this truth? …

Christ knocked for entrance but no room was made for Him ... and the light of His glory, so nigh, was withdrawn (page 734).

The God of Israel has opened the windows of heaven and sent to the world rich floods of light, but that light has been rejected (page 746).

"What sign showest thou?" ... same words spoken to me since the Minneapolis meeting. ... Now I feel no inclination to converse with the men who occupy responsible positions ... I have more freedom speaking to unbelievers than to those who hold responsible positions, and who have had so great light (pages 798, 799).

Since the General Conference of 1888, Satan has been working with special power through unconsecrated elements to weaken the confidence of God's people in the voice that has been appealing to them for these many years (page 803).

Much precious light was brought out at this meeting [Minneapolis, 1888]. ... I have heard many testimonies in all parts of the field: "I found light, precious light." "My Bible is a new Book" (page 828).

There will be those who will resist the light and crowd down those whom God has made His channels to communicate light. ... The watchmen have not kept pace with the opening providence of God, and the real heaven-sent message and messengers are scorned (page 831).

Those who do not in this place yield to the evidence God has given will war against their brethren whom God is using (page 831).

The enemy took possession of minds and their judgment was worthless, their decisions were evil, for they did not have the mind of Christ. They were doing continual injustice to the persons they talked about, and they had a demoralizing effect upon the conference (page 837).

The Lord has men of opportunity through whom He is working. From this meeting there will be decided changes in our churches. There is a faith professed but a decided want of that faith that works by love and purifies the soul (page 838).

I am warned again and again of what will be the result of this warfare you have persistently maintained against the truth (page 842).

When you stated that you had not had feelings against Eld. Waggoner, and Eld. A. T. Jones, I was surprised. Perhaps you thought thus, but how could you think thus, is a mystery to me. The feelings cherished by yourself and Elder Butler were not only despising the message, but the messengers. But the blindness of mind has come by warring against the light which the Lord designed to come to His people (page 846).

[Elder Prescott] then confessed that at the Minneapolis meeting, and since that time, he had not had altogether right feelings. He asked the forgiveness of all, and especially of Brethren Waggoner and Jones. Brother Jones, I think, was not present. He then took the arm of Brother Smith, and both went forward. Brother Smith thus made a start, but, although Brother Prescott opened the way, he did not improve the opportunity. All he said was, "the matter comes home to me; it means me" (page 862).

Oh, how I yearned in spirit for the men who, by resistance of light which God has given, have for the past two years hedged up the way that the Spirit of God shall not find access to their hearts. I heard a voice say to them, "You still are unbelieving. Stand aside or close up the ranks by coming into line and uniting in the work wholeheartedly" (page 867).

I spoke from John, chapter 15. ... Elder E. J. Waggoner followed, speaking on baptism. ... E. J. Waggoner administered the sacred ordinance to nine willing souls who felt that it was their duty to be baptized, and they were received into the church (page 874).

In their boarding places in Minneapolis [at the General Conference, Elder Smith and Brother Rupert] ... made light of the truth and of those who advocated the truth (page 875).

Elder Waggoner called and was very urgent that I should speak again to the ministerial class (page 889).

There is increased light for us ... When I see my brethren stirred with anger against God's messages and messengers, I think of similar scenes in the life of Christ and the Reformers ... treating the light sent them in the very same way that the Jews treated the light Christ brought them (page 911).

To ignore the Spirit of God, to charge it with being the spirit of the devil, placed [the Jews] in a position where God had no power to reach their hearts.

Some in Battle Creek will surely reach this point if they do not change their course. ... They are following in the path of guilt for which there can be no forgiveness, in this life or in the life to come. ... In this our day men have placed themselves where they are wholly unable to fulfil the conditions of repentance and confession; therefore they cannot find mercy and pardon. ...

The Lord has been calling His people. ... But the message and the messengers have not been received but despised. ...

In rejecting the messages given at Minneapolis, men committed sin. They have committed far greater sin by retaining for years the same hatred against God's messengers, by rejecting the truth that the Holy Spirit has been urging home (pages 912-913).

Volume Three

What pain of heart I have because of the spirit which has characterized the board meetings and councils! What a spirit has been brought into them! The ideas and opinions of one affect another, and there has been a large amount of caviling and witticism. A Witness has been in your meetings and registered it all. These weapons debase the one who uses them, but give him no victories. There has been a bringing down of sacred things to the common. Witticisms and your sharp criticisms, after the infidel style, please the devil but not the Lord. The Spirit of God has not been controlling in your councils. There have been misstatements of messengers and of the messages they bring. How dare you do it? (page 941).

There is a satanic accusing of the men who should be respected, whom God is using (page 947).

I would not now rehearse before you the evidences in the past two years of the dealings of God by His chosen servants; but the present evidence of His working is revealed to you (page 954; 1890).

Be careful how you take a position against Elder Waggoner. Have you not the best of evidence that the Lord has been communicating light through him? I have. ... (page 977).

The Lord has raised up messengers, and endued them with his Spirit ... Let no one run the risk of interposing himself between the people and the message from heaven (page 992).

You are altogether too sharp and severe toward your brethren who are younger in years, and yet whom the Lord is manifestly using to give light to His people (page 1004).

The Lord Jesus is dishonored whenever brethren of the same faith accuse another and lessen the influence of one of God's delegated messengers. The enemies of truth will make the very most of the least item by which they can excite suspicion of the men through whom God is giving light to the people. To place any obstruction in the way of this light coming to the people, will be registered as a grievous sin in the sight of God. ... Let not the influence graciously given you of God to save souls from ruin be employed in weakening the influence of others whom the Lord is using (page 1009).

You have thought that you could see inconsistencies in A. T. Jones and E. J. Waggoner. ... In the intensity of their feelings they may make mistakes; their expressions may sometimes be stronger than will impress minds favorably. But ... I know of no sins greater ... than cherishing jealousy and hatred toward ... a brother who presents a view that is not in exact harmony with their understanding of the Scriptures. Self arises, a fierce and determined spirit is aroused. They will place the brother in a position that hurts his influence ... Upon whom does the hurt come? Upon the Son of the infinite God (page 1011).

Your brethren are not as worthless rubbish, that they can be held so cheap as some have been during the past few years. In the books of heaven there are stern records to be examined, in regard to the manner in which some have dealt with the purchase of the blood of Christ (page 1012).

We should be the last people on the earth to indulge in the slightest degree the spirit of persecution against those who are bearing the message of God to the world. This is the most terrible feature of unchristlikeness that has manifested itself among us since the Minneapolis meeting.

Sometime it will be seen in its true bearing, with all the burden of woe that has resulted from it (page 1013).

We have expected than an angel is to come down from heaven, that the earth will be lightened with his glory. ... But this mighty angel comes bearing no soft, smooth message, but words that are calculated to stir the hearts of men to their very depths (page 1015).

Some may say, "I do not hate my brother; I am not as bad as that." But how little they understand their own hearts. They may think they have a zeal for God in their feelings against their brother, if his ideas seem in any way to conflict with theirs; feelings are brought to the surface that have no kinship with love. They show no disposition to harmonize with him. They would as lief be at swords' point with their brother as not. And yet he may be bearing a message from God to the people— just the light they need for this time (page 1022).

Will the Lord's messenger bear the pressure brought against him? If so, it is because God bids him stand in his strength and vindicate the truth that is sent of God (page 1023).

When the truth is presented by one who is himself sanctified through it, it has a freshness, a force, that gives it a convincing power to the hearer. The truth, in its power upon the heart, is precious, and the truth addressed to the understanding is clear. Both are needful—the word and the inward testimony of the Spirit (page 1024).

There has been a determined effort to make of no effect the message God has sent (page 1024).

Should the Lord's messengers, after standing manfully for the truth for a time, fall under temptation, and dishonor Him who has given them their work, will that be proof that the message is not true? No, because the Bible is true (page 1025).

I ask, What means the contention and strife among us? What means this harsh, iron spirit, which is seen in our churches and in our institutions, and which is so utterly unchristlike? I have deep sorrow of heart because I have seen how readily a word or action of Elder Jones or Elder Waggoner is criticized. How readily many minds overlook all the good that has been done through them in the few years past, and see no evidence that God is working through these instrumentalities (page 1026).

The Lord has given abundance of evidence in messages of light and salvation. No more tender calls, no better opportunities, could be given them in order that they might do that which they ought to have done at Minneapolis. The light has been withdrawing from some, and ever since they have walked in sparks of their own kindling (page 1030).

The levity of some, the free speeches of others, the manner of treating the messenger and the message when in their private stopping places, the spirit that stirred to action from beneath, all stand registered in the books of heaven (page 1031).

Men have done so much harm in their blindness, working against the messengers and messages God has sent, that I fear it would be a great mistake to reward them by giving them positions of trust as true men to be depended upon (page 1034).

Avoid all impressions which savor of extremes; for those who are watching for a chance will seize hold of any words strongly expressed to justify them in their feelings of calling you an extremist (page 1038).

Then let not the chosen of God be found in opposition to the messengers and messages He sends ... not against brethren, not against the Lord's anointed (page 1038).

Some have made confession. ... Others have made no confession, for they were too proud to do this, and they have not come to the light. They were moved at the meeting by another spirit, and they knew not that God had sent these young men, Elders Jones and Waggoner, to bear a special message to them, which they treated with ridicule and contempt, not realizing that the heavenly intelligences were looking upon them and registering their words in the books of heaven (page 1043).

The people of God have had an opportunity to see what is the work these agents are doing, and yet those who are opposed to the points of truth which they brought out will, if occasion affords them a chance, make it appear that they are not in harmony with them, as much as to say, Beware of what they teach, for they carry matters to the extreme; they are not safe men (page 1044).

I pray that these men upon whom God has laid the burden of a solemn work may be able to give the trumpet a certain sound, and honor God at every step, and that their path at every step may grow brighter and brighter, until the close of time (page 1045).

The more closely we walk with Christ, the center of all love and light, the greater will be our affection for His lightbearers. ... You cannot love God and yet fail to love your brethren (page 1049).

We should pray not only that laborers may be sent forth into the great harvest field, but that we may have a clear conception of truth, so that when the messengers of truth shall come we may accept the message and respect the messenger (page 1050).

Both message and messenger have been held in doubt by those who should have been the first to discern and act upon it as the word of God (page 1051).

Fear to ridicule the message or the messenger (page 1052).

The true Christian will fear to make light of God's message, lest he may lay a stumbling block in the way of a soul (page 1052).

The message given us by A. T. Jones, and E. J. Waggoner is the message of God to the Laodicean church (page 1052).

The many and confused ideas in regard to Christ's righteousness and justification by faith are the result of the position you have taken toward the man and the message sent of God (page 1053).

Why take so much account of that which may appear to you as objectionable in the messenger, and sweep away all the evidences that God has given to balance the mind in regard to the truth? (page 1060).

No one who has enlisted to serve God will be free from temptation. Satan will say, "Do not be carried away with any whimsical notion. Do not work like a slave unless you are well paid for it" (page 1064).

You [nephew, Frank] did unite with those who resisted the Spirit of God. You had all the evidence that you needed that the Lord was working through Brethren Jones and Waggoner; but you did not receive the light ... that these men had a message from God, and you had made light of both message and messengers (page 1066).

Never before have I seen among our people such self-complacency and unwillingness to accept and acknowledge light as was manifested at Minneapolis. I have been shown that not one of the company who cherished the spirit manifested at that meeting would again have clear light to discern the preciousness of the truth sent them from heaven until they humbled their pride and confessed that they were not actuated by the Spirit of God. ... They were actuated by the same spirit that inspired Korah, Dathan, and Abiram. ... [The angel of the Lord said] "The people are acting over the rebellion of Korah, Dathan, and Abiram. ... It is not you [Ellen White] they are despising, but the messengers and the message I send to My people. They have shown their contempt for the word of the Lord" (pages 1067-1068).

God meant that the watchmen should arise and with united voices send forth a decided message. ... Then the strong, clear light of that other angel who comes down from heaven having great power, would have filled the earth with his glory ... the very message that God meant should go forth from the Minneapolis meeting ... heavenly messengers have grieved, impatient at the delay ... message of truth which angels of heaven were seeking to communicate through human agencies— justification by faith, the righteousness of Christ (pages 1070-1071).

The loud cry of the third angel has already begun in the revelation of the righteousness of Christ (page 1073).

I have felt so sorry that you could not recognize the voice of Jesus, the true Shepherd. The Lord has wrought out the demonstration of truth before your eyes, yet you did not see, and your heart was not submitted to the leadings of the Holy Spirit of God (page 1084).

God may choose instrumentalities that we do not accept, because they do not exactly meet our ideas. ... Then begins the dissecting of character (page 1091).

Why question and find fault with one another? Why misinterpret and misconstrue the words and acts of your brethren? Is there no better work for you to do than to discourage one another and try to put out the light of your brethren? (page 1095).

I had hoped that the truth which has been shining in clear, distinct beams of light since the Minneapolis meeting, would flood your soul (page 1106).

After this he saw in the Review the articles of Brother A. T. Jones in regard to the image of the beast, and then the one from Elder Smith presenting the opposite view. He was perplexed and troubled. He had received much light and comfort in reading articles from Brethren Jones and Waggoner; but here was one of the old laborers, one who had written many of our standard books, and whom we had believed to be taught of God, who seemed to be in conflict with Brother Jones (page 1119).

We are not to spurn the message nor the messengers by whom God shall send light to His people (page 1121).

Those who opposed Brethren Jones and Waggoner manifested no disposition to meet them like brethren, and with the Bible in hand consider prayerfully and in a Christlike spirit the points of difference (page 1122).

Brother Jones has been giving the message for this time—meat in due season for the starving flock of God (page 1122).

Brother Jones seeks to arouse the professed people of God from their death-like slumber. ... Instantly Brother Gage is aroused; he harnesses for the battle, and before the congregation in the tabernacle he takes his position in opposition to Brother Jones. Was this in the order of God? Did the Spirit of the Lord go from Brother Jones and inspire Brother Gage to do this work? (pages 1122-1123).

"Who required this at your hand, to rise up against the message and the messengers I sent to My people with light, with grace and power? Why have you lifted up your souls against God? Why did you block the way with your own perverse spirit? And afterward when evidence was piled upon evidence, why did you not humble your hearts before God, and repent of your rejection of the message of mercy He sent you?" (page 1126).

The power of every mind ... is to be employed, not to hedge up the way before the messages God sends to His people (page 1127).

[These brethren] might have been God's instruments to carry the work forward with power; but their influence was exerted to counteract the Lord's message, to make the work appear questionable. Every jot and tittle of this will have to be repented of (page 1128).

The opposition in our own ranks has imposed upon the Lord's messengers a laborious and soul trying task, for they have had to meet difficulties and obstacles which need not have existed (page 1128).

The influence that grew out of the resistance of light and truth at Minneapolis tended to make of no effect the light God had given to His people through the Testimonies (page 1129).

In the blessings that have since accompanied the presentation of the truth, justification by faith and the imputed righteousness of Christ, they have not discerned increased evidence from God as to where and how He is and has been working (page 1136).

You have but in a partial way been in harmony with the work that brethren Jones and Waggoner have under God been doing to bring up the church to understand their true state and come to the supper prepared for them (page 1137).

"Why did you not accept the message I sent through My servants? Why did you watch those men to find something to question and doubt, when you should have accepted the message that bore the imprint of the Most High?" (page 1138).

Can you not discern who has the message to give to the people for this time? (page 1139).

Think you, my brother, if the Lord has raised up men to give to the world a message to the people to prepare them to stand in the great day of God, that any one could by their influence stop the work and close the mouth of the messengers? No (page 1140).

Is the work that has been going on since the Minneapolis meeting of God? If not, it is of another spirit. ... I know that the Lord is in this work (page 1141).

He saw the articles by Elder Jones on the formation of the image, and was greatly blessed in reading them. Then came Elder Smith's article opposed to Elder Jones. This brought him into trial just before the week of prayer (page 1143).

We must not disparage the Lord's message or his messengers (page 1146).

My brother, I am not pleased to have you feel as you do in regard to Brethren Waggoner, Jones, and Prescott. Had these men had the cooperation of our ministering brethren, and had they drawn in even cords, the work would be years in advance of what it is now. It is not pleasing to the Lord for you to retain the feelings you do in these matters.

These men [Jones and Waggoner] are working in their line and must attend to the duties of their section of the work, which is of immense responsibility (page 1147).

The course which has been pursued toward Elder Jones has been an offense to God (page 1156).

We have every evidence that the Lord is using Elder Jones, Elder Waggoner, and Professor Prescott; and with this evidence before us, it pains my heart that any of my brothers in the faith should feel impatient and bitter toward them, and refuse to draw in cords of love and unity with them (page 1156).

Brethren Prescott, Jones, and Waggoner are fallible. You are fully as fallible. They may err in some points. You also may err in some points (page 1158).

The Lord has raised up Brother Jones and Brother Waggoner to proclaim a message to the world to prepare a people to stand in the day of God (page 1208b).

Light from heaven has been called excitement. … We must be very careful not to grieve the Holy Spirit of God, in pronouncing the ministration of His Holy Spirit a species of fanaticism (page 1210).

I have been afraid, terribly afraid[,] that those who felt the bright beams of the Sun of righteousness … will come to the conclusion that God's heaven-sent blessings are a delusion (page 1212).

I am indeed sorry both for brother Prescott and brother Jones. I have felt very anxious in regard to them both, but especially in regard to Bro. Jones who is so ardent in his faith, and does not manifest the caution he should in his statements by pen or voice. I did pray that these dear brethren would be so completely hid in Christ Jesus, that they would not make one misstep. I have more confidence in them today than I have had in the past, and fully believe that God will be their helper, their comfort and their hope (page 1240; 1894).

Keep the heart with all diligence lest by one unwise impulse, we shall grieve and distress one of the Lord's chosen messengers. "Touch not mine anointed, and do my prophets no harm" (page 1241).

Bro. Jones and Prescott are the Lord's chosen messengers, beloved of God. They have cooperated with God in the work for this time. ... These brethren are God's ambassadors. They have been quick to catch the bright beams of the Sun of Righteousness, and have responded by imparting the heavenly light to others (pages 1241-1242).

Let every soul who has received the theory of the truth now take heed how they treat God's messengers. Let no one be found working on Satan's side of the question, as an accuser of the brethren (page 1242).

[Some] will exalt the messenger above the message, ... forgetting that it is God working wondrously through him for His own name's glory (page 1244).

They should give glory to God because they see through the interpretation of the word from the lips of the messenger, marvelous things out of the living oracles (page 1244).

Some will ask why it is that these messengers who fed us with the bread from heaven, should make a mistake? ... Men who have been chosen of God to do a special work have been imperiled because the people have looked to the men in the place of looking to God (pages 1244-1245).

The Lord has chosen men to bear light and messages of great importance to the people in these last days (page 1245).

Every inch of the ground had to be fought in presenting the present message, and some have not been reconciled with the providence of God in selecting the very men whom He did select to bear this special message. They ask, Why it is that He has not chosen men who have been long in the work? ... God has chosen the very men He wanted, and we have reason to thank Him that these men have carried forward the work with faithfulness, and have been the mouthpiece for God (page 1245).

Those men [Jones and Waggoner] are chosen of the Lord (page 1246).

Did the men who have thus been warned step quickly into the path that was marked out for them, as these two brethren have done? No, they did not (page 1246).

... because the chosen of God have been too ardent in their ideas (page 1247).

Let those men who have not received the draught from the wells of salvation ... (page 1247).

... with the men who were chosen to give the message which the people needed in these last days (page 1247).

... these men whom God was using (page 1247).

The chosen agents of God ... (page 1247).

... faithful watchmen (page 1248).

... men who have born the message of God (page 1248).

... the Lord ... has given them their message (page 1248).

... men to whom God has given the message of truth to give to the world at this time (page 1249).

... brethren who have been doing His work (page 1249).

... message God has given (page 1249)

Those who are content with the form of godliness exclaim "Be careful, do not go to extremes" (page 1251).

The very men whom God has entrusted with a message for His people have not been treated with respect (page 1299).

... the message and the messengers (page 1300).

... the men who have borne this gospel message (page 1300).

You have had a hatred of the message which His chosen messengers have proclaimed, (page 1300).

... the messengers and message God has sent (page 1303).

... the message or the messengers (page 1309).

… God's delegated servants (page 1309).

The heaven sent message was truth (page 1309).

Yet many have listened to the truth spoken in demonstration of the Spirit, and they have not only refused to accept the message, but they have hated the light (page 1336).

The Lord in His great mercy sent a most precious message to His people through Elders Waggoner and Jones (page 1336).

This is the very work which the Lord designs that the message He has given His servants shall perform in the heart and mind of every human agent (page 1339).

God gave His messengers just what the people needed (page 1339).

How long will you hate and despise the messengers of God's righteousness? (page 1341).

… whom the Lord recognized as His servants (page 1341).

You will see that these men whom you have spoken against (page 1342).

Christ's delegated messengers (page 1342).

Why do you cherish such bitterness against Elder A. T. Jones and Elder Waggoner? (page 1353).

God has given Brother Jones and Brother Waggoner a message for the people. You do not believe that God has upheld them, but He has given them precious light, and their message has fed the people of God. When you reject the message borne by these men, you reject Christ, the Giver of the message (page 1353).

Volume Four

… the messages God has been giving His people (page 1395).

They have chosen contempt for both the messenger and the message, from the time Eld. Jones and Waggoner were given a special work to do for these last days (page 1395).

… the messages God sends (page 1395).

I am sure from the light given me of God, the men, some of them who are the main movers in Battle Creek in councils, first need to confess to God their rejection of the messengers and the message He hath sent (page 1410).

The righteousness of Christ by faith has been ignored (page 1436).

These men have hated the messenger and the messages God has given him to proclaim (page 1473).

Some felt annoyed at this outpouring, and their own natural dispositions were manifested. They said, This is only excitement; it is not the Holy Spirit, not showers from heaven of the latter rain. ... Those who resisted the Spirit of God at Minneapolis were waiting for a chance to travel over the same ground again. ...

They pronounced in their heart and soul and words that this manifestation of the Holy Spirit was fanaticism and delusion. They stood like a rock, the waves of mercy flowing upon and around them, but beaten back by their hard and wicked hearts, which resisted the Holy Spirit's working. ... disgraceful treatment of Jesus Christ, represented by the Holy Spirit. Had Christ been before them, they would have treated Him in a manner similar to that in which the Jews treated Christ (pages 1478-1479).

The Spirit of the Lord has been upon His messengers whom He hath sent with light, precious light (page 1485).

Here is the secret of the movements made to oppose the men whom God sent with a message of blessing for His people. These men have been hated, the message was despised, as verily as Christ himself was hated and despised at His first advent. Men in responsible positions have manifested the very attributes that Satan has revealed (page 1525).

Finite men have been warring against God and the truth and the Lord's chosen messengers, counterworking them by every means they dared to use (page 1526).

... the very men whom God has used to present light and truth which His people needed (page 1526).

Men have come to Battle Creek who have been accompanied by the

Holy Spirit; but unless they fought every inch of ground over and over again, in seeking to maintain correct methods, they were at last overborne (page 1535).

Some have treated the Spirit as an unwelcome guest, refusing to receive the rich gift, refusing to acknowledge it, turning from it, and condemning it as fanaticism. ... The light that is to lighten the whole earth with its glory was resisted, and by the action of our own brethren has been in a great degree kept away from the world, (page 1575)

They have ridiculed, mocked, and derided God's servants who have borne to them the message of mercy from heaven (page 1642).

The work has been carried forward in Christ's lines (page 1651).

Men professing godliness have despised Christ in the person of His messengers. Like the Jews, they reject God's message (page 1651).

You hated the messages sent from heaven. You manifested against Christ a prejudice of the very same character and more offensive to God than that of the Jewish nation (page 1656).

You refused to admit the truth of the heaven-sent message (page 1656).

You have most powerful truth to present (page 1756)

Your suppositions regarding the position and work of Elders A. T. Jones and E. J. Waggoner were incorrect (page 1759).

More "good news" books by Robert J. Wieland are available from the publisher. Please contact CFI Book Publishers at P.O. Box 159, Gordonsville, Tennessee 38563

The Good News Is Better Than You Think

Powerful Good News

Oro afinado en fuego (Spanish: *Gold Tried in the Fire*)

La Buona Novella (Italian: *The Glad Tidings*)